THROUGH KINGDOM EYES

JIM VAN RITE

To order additional copies of this book, contact:

Simply Best Reads LLC
39-67 58th Street, 1st floor
Woodside, NY 11377, USA
Phone: (+1 888-203-7688)
simplybestreads.com

TABLE OF CONTENTS

PROFILE: Jim Van Rite -- VII

BEGINNING AND THESIS --- XI

CHAPTER 1
My Story, My Need for "Kingdom Eyes" ------------------------------1
CHILDHOOD --1
YOUNG ADULT --2
VIETNAM--2
ENTERTAINER--2
BEGINNING IN MINISTRY--4
MARRIAGE---5
ALCOHOLICS ANONYMOUS-----------------------------------5
LEAVING THE MINISTRY ------------------------------------6
FAMILY--7
AFTER DIVORCE FROM FIRST WIFE ---------------------8
THE KEY TO THE KEY --------------------------------------- 10

CHAPTER 2
Why the Need for Kingdom Eyes? ------------------------------- 13
MY THEOLOGICAL BASE------------------------------------- 13
SCIENCE AND REALITY ------------------------------------- 20
WHO IS GOD? AND WHO AM I? ------------------------- 23
THE KINGDOM OF GOD------------------------------------- 27
KINGDOM EYES --- 31

CHAPTER 3
The Bible and Kingdom Eyes ------------------------------------- 35
THE BIBLE AS CONVERSATION WITH GOD------------------ 35
THE BIBLE AS A LOVE LETTER FROM GOD TO HIS CHILDREN------------------ 41
THE BIBLE AS A CHALLENGE FROM GOD TO HIS CHILDREN------------------ 43

CHAPTER 4
Living in the Now with Kingdom Eyes ------------------------- 50
EXAMPLES OF KINGDOM EYES ----------------------------- 50
THE EXAMPLE OF AIDAN ----------------------------------- 51
RESPONSE TO HOLY ISLAND AND LIFESTYLE TODAY ----------------- 52
"REALITY"--- 54
FORGIVENESS --- 55

Looking Back to Look Forward -- 56
Reflections on Ministry at Martin UMC --- 61
Difficulties for Living the Kingdom of God on Earth -------------------- 62
Reflections on a Past Time -- 65
Concluding Thoughts: Some Things That Have Changed in Me ----- 67

CHAPTER 5
The Kingdom Effect: A Giver; Not a Taker Be ------------------------------- 73

CONCLUSION --- 82

PROFILE

JIM VAN RITE

I am an ordained United Methodist elder (retired). My BS degree is from Texas Wesleyan University (then Texas Wesleyan College), and my MDiv is from Brite Divinity School at TCU.

My book is about my spiritual development and how I came to understand that the kingdom of God is not only promised in this world, but that we are commanded to come to God in love, as Jesus loves us.

My problem was that I didn't know how to love anyone, including myself. The book begins with me speaking of that.

Yet God clearly called me to ministry, and I just as clearly told him that a man unable to love had no place trying to be a pastor to his sheep.

I spent ten years as a full-time UMC pastor, with some success, but my family was in disarray. I chose to take "honorable location" while I would work out the family problems. Divorce came anyway, and I was out of the church professionally for twenty-five years. God never stopped moving in my life, and this book was always calling to me because of him.

As my second wife, Sue, and I got together, I began to teach Sunday school at St. Andrews UMC in Arlington, Texas. I call Sue Suzie, and both of us felt the hand of God in our meeting.

I had just learned that God would not point a celestial finger at me and make me love. Rather, I got the message that I would have to risk saying that word, and then I would have to do acts of love and kindness in order to begin to get the feelings.

I heard this as a tenant of AA, "Feelings follow action," and I decided that if it worked for others, it just might work for me. It did.

We moved to Hurst, Texas, at a time when I felt a great need to surrender to God in a more complete way, and when I was offered the position of associate pastor at Martin UMC in Bedford, Texas, I took it.

I understood that spiritual growth would come through sharing in love with the congregants of that church and others.

My role there was teaching and visitation, as well as participating in the worship services.

Six years later, I retired again, and the love Suzie and I were showered with was just stupendous. I told folks there that I was neither right nor left in my understanding of the gospels, but that I was a seeker of spiritual closeness to God and his children. I said that spiritual growth came through, risking to love as much like Jesus as we could as we journeyed in him.

I made great strides in this direction, and for the first time since seminary, writing a book became possible. I knew and could share love, and others felt that also. I could write about Jesus's call to perfection as God is perfect and know that slowly the Holy Spirit was guiding me in that direction. I understood Paul speaking of "working out our salvation in fear and trembling" to mean truly giving up my will to God. It was something I had feared and fought for years, yet people at Martin saw me as loving, and I knew it was God and not me.

My professor of New Testament at Texas Wesleyan reappeared in my life at just this time, and he agreed to proofread the book and to help me put it in order.

A brief synopsis: in the Lord's Prayer, Jesus prays, "Your kingdom come. Your will be done, on earth as it is in heaven." I take it seriously, that this means we Christians are called to help this to happen and to do it through offering love to others in the name of Jesus.

In John 9:39, Jesus says, "I came into this world for judgment so that those who do not see may see, and those who do see may become blind."

In Luke 6:25, Jesus says that those who are laughing now will mourn, and Matthew 20:16 says, "So the last will be first, and the first will be last."

As I understand these words and Jesus's call for us to be perfect as our Father in heaven is (Matthew 5:48) as a call to turn this world upside down, we are called to do the love he calls for as a commandment in John 13:34, and together this and his attention to the poor and dispossessed (Luke 4:18) tell us that our worldly values can never lead us to him. We put ourselves first in almost everything as a matter of survival. But Jesus calls us to put the kingdom first (Matthew 6:33) and that then we will see God. ("Blessed are the pure in heart, for they will see God" [Matthew 5:8].)

The inventor of the atomic bomb, Robert Oppenheimer wrote, "Now I am become death, the destroyer of worlds." I believe we are called to become "love." This book is my journey into love and what I came to believe along the way. On my journey, I began to understand that the spiritual sightedness that Jesus speaks of in John 9:39 is about seeing the kingdom way of living now, i.e., "kingdom eyes." Those who see or have their sight restored (as in Luke 4:18) see their lives and the responsibilities of living in a Christlike way as possible—even if still step by step.

BEGINNING AND THESIS

God is serious about love. This is clear when we read the great commandment and Jesus's only commandment in John 13. Like I said, he is serious about love, and especially that we should learn to love "as he loves us."

So it is my purpose in this book to explore how we should attempt to live in response to his clear call on us to love in this way, and along the way, I will share some of the reasons we find it hard to envision doing so.

CHAPTER 1

MY STORY,
MY NEED FOR "KINGDOM EYES"

CHILDHOOD

I was about five years old and sitting in the back seat of a car driven by my aunt Margie. Mom was on the front passenger side, and my younger brother, Kent, and cousin Danny were in the back seat with me. Some sort of group conversation was going on, and I was expected to give a response, but I missed the cue. My mother said, as a broadcast to all in the car, "Jimmy is always in a world of his own."

Years later, I heard my dad say that he was never lonely because his mind always kept him entertained. That was me, too, and in many ways, my mind is still going all of the time. Unfortunately, I got something else from my dad. Dad didn't really know how to express his feelings to others, and in fact, he didn't really know how to trust and love others very well. No doubt this came from living on his own with his brother when they were ten and twelve years old. His home wasn't safe, so they got an adult to rent an apartment in his name, which they then paid for from their employment as newsboys for the *Shreveport Journal* newspaper.

Our family was dysfunctional in the extreme; and yes, I withdrew and didn't get the love thing either.

In the third going into the fourth grade, I discovered the Tom Swift series of books, and then the Hardy Boys. And I read all of them that year. I was off and running, and I read all of the science fiction books in our small community library in the foreign staff colony in Aruba. By the end of the sixth grade, I was reading adult novels, such as *The Robe* by Lloyd C. Douglass and other Christian historical novels. Reading was my escape, and although I did have friends who, like me, were on the fringes of our childhood peer society, books kept me entertained more than anything else.

YOUNG ADULT

As an adult, I became more of a loner but was always looking for that perfect woman to make me feel okay. When I did get together with a new woman, I didn't have the emotional tools to keep the relationship growing, and so I would be a loner again.

VIETNAM

Shortly after graduation from high school, I joined the US Marines. I served two separate tours: one from November 1960 to November 1963, and after a couple of years, I went back in to serve in Vietnam. On that second tour, from May 1965 to May 1968, I quickly found myself in Da Nang, Vietnam. I wasn't in a direct combat role there, so I had lots of time on my hand, and I spent that time in search of meaning in my life. I broke up my eighteen-month tour with several rest and relaxation weeks away in the region, plus one back home, but that still left me with a lot of time in the country.

It was there that I began to read books about meditation and Christian meditation. I didn't necessarily believe in God, as in having faith in him, but I did believe he existed. Meditating in him opened doors in me and, while nothing big happened then, it was those opened doors that swung wider open in my last days as an entertainer.

After my tour with the marines, I held a couple of jobs. Then in my mid-twenties, I was laid off from LTV Aerospace in Grand Prairie. The company had a fund set aside by contract for laid-off workers. This weekly amount was combined with unemployment, and the result was called sub-pay. It wasn't much, but it allowed me to begin a music career.

ENTERTAINER

I played guitar and sang in nightclubs, working my way up to nicer hotel bars where rooms and board were a part of my pay. It was during this time that I began to talk to God about my lifestyle. All my relationships with women failed, and I knew that it was about my discomfort with someone saying "I love you" to me. When I heard those words, I felt I was expected to also express those feelings, and I didn't have them. There was an empty spot there in my heart (if I had one), and I would break things off because of my discomfort.

My last gig lasted for almost two years and began with a hotel chain's Houston location. I was living with a woman in Arlington, playing all week in Houston, and then coming home for Sunday and Monday.

At this time, my dad began to have heart problems that resulted in a heart attack and four bypasses. Now, I was flying back to be with him and my family during this crisis. A significant thing happened as Dad slipped into a deadly cycle of medications fighting each other. Drugs to keep his heart beating regularly were causing his lungs to fill with fluid. When they worked on getting his lungs okay, his heart would again slip into a ragged rhythm. The doctors said that Dad's life was in God's hands, for they were out of options.

My mother and Dad were not close, so I was surprised at how hard she took the news. Nevertheless, my brothers, my sister, Mom, and I moved by common consent to the chapel at Harris Hospital in downtown Fort Worth. My prayer was for Mom to be okay, as I assumed at that time that Dad was not going to make it.

Something happened there that still causes me pause. I felt a warmth come over me in such a complete way—like nothing I had ever felt before nor since. I have sometimes compared it to being in a giant wave in the surf, for I was completely helpless in its grip, and yet there was nothing to be afraid of. In the warmth that took me over, I heard or sensed the words "It will be okay." That's all, just those words.

My brothers, sister, and Mom had their own experiences, but the result was that Dad had an after-death experience. He made it to heaven and had a joyous reunion with others, only to be called back to this world. He later said that it was hard on him. He really wanted to stay.

I had been praying for Mom to be okay, for it seemed that the thought of losing Dad was more than she could bear. This, even though their relationship had been rocky for a while. However, as he recovered, she became his caregiver. That was a role for her that seemed to work better for both of them. For me, this was the beginning of my new relationship with God and, looking back, the beginning of my call to ministry.

I was going to a Christian church near the hotel I was playing at, andI was whining to God about the vast emptiness that was in my life. I hated my lifestyle as an entertainer. I wasn't going to be top shelf in my field, and I knew it. I could keep playing for the company that had sent me there from Houston, or I could find another. I was, after all, very employable at that level, but again the lifestyle was just empty and devoid of any real meaning.

I recalled my experience at the hospital with Dad, and I turned to God for help. It was then that I began to do meditative prayer in my hotel room. I just wanted to get some sort of sign from God. That sign came in a big way, but the telling of that experience needs to wait for more context as this book evolves. In fact, it wasn't a single experience anyway, but a series of things—spiritual happenings— that clearly amounted to a call to Christian ministry that occurred over the next few months.

BEGINNING IN MINISTRY

I waffled and tried to tell God that I wasn't able to love, so why would he want me as a pastor to his sheep? I clearly wasn't qualified.

Months later, after completing a license to preach course, I was a newly minted and licensed-to-preach United Methodist pastor. I had eight years of college and seminary ahead of me, but I was assigned three churches in Palo Pinto County at which to begin my journey into ministry. I could say much about that learning experience for me and for the folks I ministered to, and I will through these pages, but the thing that stands out the most about those folks was that they were used to "raising preachers" and told me so.

As for myself, I was immediately angry with God, and I would rail at him often that in my understanding he had promised to teach me to love, and in that area, I had not changed. I could fake it, but, and in truth, those wonderful folks made it easy—yet I didn't feel it.

Secondly, I heard two things from God in the midst of my anger, and I don't know exactly how I heard these; I just did. First, I learned that his love was sufficient, and that we would eventually get me there; and secondly and most confusing to me at first, was that he needed us as much as we needed him. The most amazing thing was that I could be angry with him, and he would still love me.

I have come to understand the first of these in this way: we are only here to learn to love him, ourselves, and others as much as he loves us. All else is just what we do in the meantime, and if we understand "the parable of the pearl of great price," then we will learn along the way to put God first in all things. Seminary taught me something else about this: that if we truly hear God, then we must act on what we hear, or we didn't really hear God in the first place.

MARRIAGE

I hadn't been in Palo Pinto long when a woman I had met on a blind date while I was still living near the Texas Wesleyan campus was suddenly in my life in a big way. She had been praying for a husband and me for a wife, and we both felt that our coming together was an answer to our common prayers. There wasn't a whole lot of romance involved, and when her rent house in Justin, Texas, was narrowly missed by a tornado, I proposed, and we got married.

That marriage ultimately lasted sixteen years, and we had one child, a boy, together, but it taught me much about myself and propelled me further down the path of learning to love.

ALCOHOLICS ANONYMOUS

She felt a need to enter the rooms of AA, and after a time in Al Anon, I moved into those rooms for my past drinking while I was entertaining. I learned a lot about honesty in those rooms as people opened up in ways I had never seen before. The premise for such honesty was a preamble that most meetings began with. We confessed that we would be ruthlessly honest and work as hard at sobriety as we had at drinking. The not-drinking part was easy for me as I had just drunk on stage as a tool to get me loose. That, and drinking because of self-hatred, actually qualified me for AA. Self-hatred is just another facet of a lack of self-esteem, and I had to admit that as I looked at all my failures to that date—failure to keep my family together, failure to succeed in ministry because of the distraction of my marriage, and, just as much, failure because of a lack of a sense of urgency in any part of my life—I could see a deep-seated lack of self-esteem in me. I was a drifter in life, still partially living in the dream world my mom had tagged me with as a five-year-old.

I suppose that my lack of urgency was a result of my defenses against being hurt, and it fed my low self-esteem. Often someone in AA would say that they had to drink in order to be somebody. When I drank onstage, it was to be that entertainer that I could not be when sober. I had tight control over what I would let you see of me. Hiding from you caused me to hide from myself and re-enforced my world where I was okay—even when I wasn't okay.

LEAVING THE MINISTRY

Early into the Al Anon meetings, I took leave from the active ministry to try and save my marriage and family, but it was to no avail. Lou and I separated and divorced, and I was left to work on the why of it all— especially my part.

A funny thing happened, as the old jokes say. I was railing at God again at night now, and yet in the mornings, I would wake up feeling refreshed and enabled by him to face the day. God was my therapist. He let me exhaust myself and spend my anger against him; and then, as I finally slept with my anger slated, he healed me in stages. That time lasted a few months, and then the need to be angry ran its course. I wasn't healed, but my healing would enter a new stage a few years down the road.

FAMILY

This is a good place for me to talk about my two boys—now men— who are the fruit of that marriage. One, Jeremy, my stepson, told me recently that his defenses are just as mine used to be. He dismisses those who don't care for him and doesn't know how to love a woman or let her love him.

He said he didn't know how to be friends with someone to whom he was attracted, and I said that love without a base in friendship isn't love at all but some form of either lust or a need to possess a trophy to make oneself feel okay. I was sharing out of my memory of my own self-caused misery.

Jeremy is my stepson, but I have raised him as my own and, with his natural father's permission, even changed his last name to mine. Today he wears my name with love, for when I asked him who did he know who loves him, he said it was me and his daughter. He is working through the same problems with love that I did, and my life today is modeling a better way of being a man than I did when he was young.

My natural son, Joshua, picked up my love for reading, and you could say that the books have shaped him. We both read hundreds of science fiction books which, if you take the message from all of them, are a pretty good lesson in the humanities. This is true because the best of science fiction focuses on the human condition: what makes us who we are and why we seek to find ourselves by expanding our horizons.

From time to time, Josh will stop and thank me for putting books in his hands at an early age. There is a country song, "The House That Built Me"; Josh and I could both say to some extent there were books that helped to build us. We both wanted and still want so much for humanity, and much of that came as we lived through the characters of science fiction books and, for me, also the Christian novels of my grade school and junior high days.

I am proud of my boys today for both are successful in their fields of work, and both continue to thank me for giving them direction. The irony of that is I was just faking it to make it and spouting God-given wisdom that was above my ability to live. Yet God never stopped working on me, and even as I struggled with love and self-esteem, some good work for my boys and others was accomplished through my relationship with my Savior, Jesus Christ.

My dad never told me he loved me until we exchanged "I love you" in the last year of his life. I was determined to break the cycle of being insulated from our feelings even then, and as a result, my boys have never had a conversation with me when I didn't tell them that I love them. That, too, has been a part of my education by God on how to love.

It was God in me urging me to risk a new behavior that has changed me over time, and God is urging Jeremy to risk the same by sharing his own problems with love with me. His mother and I often fought loudly for our own selfish purposes in front of them. We modeled so much of what is wrong in relationships. Now I get to model love for my new wife, Suzie, and others in a way that he can see and use as he will.

Josh has his own family and is working with God in his own way to show love to those he holds close. He, too, has trust issues, but in time God and my better example are helping both him and his family to heal.

AFTER DIVORCE FROM FIRST WIFE

So, after my first wife, the boys' mother, and I divorced, a few years passed before I met a woman who would never be free from an abusive relationship, but nevertheless, we flirted with the impossible.

I had always expected God to somehow make me able to love, but what I learned in this mostly on-the-phone relationship was that I was going to have to risk saying those words and then acting in loving ways for my heart to be changed. In AA, they say "Feelings follow action," and I found that to work when it came to love. Saying "I love you," and then acting out of love slowly warmed my heart. That relationship had no chance of surviving, but by letting God lead me through the fear of committing myself to a relationship with someone, I began to receive the promise of being able to love.

It was then that God could move in a big way in my life. I was out of the active ministry and not even attending church when a retired pastor I knew brought his car in for service at a Toyota dealership where I worked. He said to me that I was not living up to the beliefs that he had always heard me express when we had talked in earlier years. At the same time, it seemed that everywhere I turned people were calling me a lone wolf and an outsider by choice. It was then that God brought me another vision.

I was sitting in my office at the dealership, and maybe I was daydreaming, when suddenly I was looking at a woman's profile. This happening was like a daydream, but I could hear God informing me in some way that she was just right for me.

As a result of my being called to account by my pastor friend and by this vision, I started to look for a church to attend, and within the month, I met that woman in real life. I met her at a karaoke show where I would occasionally sing and we would talk. Well, I would talk and she would listen, make comments, and ask lots of questions.

I was also singing one-man shows at retirement centers, VFWs, and American Legion halls at the time, and she would come and be there to listen to me. We were obviously becoming friends, but I felt protective toward her when it came to me and my inability to go any further with our relationship. So I told her that she was moving too fast, and then one night I told her that she couldn't love me because she couldn't love herself. (Have you ever heard the one about when you point a finger at someone, you are pointing three back at yourself?)

Her response was nothing like I expected, and it was the one thing for which I had no defense. She said, "Let me love you as I can." It was an emotional, spiritual trap for me, and I felt the hand of God in it. This was that moment when I realized that she was the one I had seen in the vision, and I couldn't walk away. I was at the moment of forever, and I knew it. I didn't really have to think; I just said "okay," and I resolved to do all that I needed to do to love her. We really began our journey that night. Her name is Sue, but I call her Suzie, and she has her own story of how she came to that night, but it is all about God preparing her for that moment also.

I moved in that night, and during the night, I had a dream/vision of her and me going on to eternity together. I woke up with one question on my mind: could she really learn to trust and love herself, and then me? God calmed my fears as a simple thought entered my head. He had brought us this far, and he would be with us always. We could do it together.

THE KEY TO THE KEY

Now back to my family of origin. When my father was still a preteen, his home became too dangerous for him and his brother. Their mother was mentally ill and unable to take care of them or protect them from her boyfriends. Dad's older brother, known as June, arranged with a man who worked with them at the *Shreveport Journal,* a newspaper, to rent a room for them in a seedy hotel in his name.

The boys sold newspapers to support themselves and were doing reasonably well when their situation was discovered by truant officers. They were sent to a reform school only because Louisiana had no foster care in the 1920s. They would have remained there until grown. They had no close relatives to come and rescue them. However, they were later rescued by distant relatives, but they were separated into different homes. Nevertheless, they remained close throughout their lives.

I tell this story to talk about love. My father was not one to demonstrate whatever affection that he may have felt for my younger brother and me, and I have only vague memories of him showing Mom affection during our growing-up years.

In the year that he died, I walked into his sick room, and with head down and feet shuffling, I told him that I loved him. Then for the first time in my life, he told me loved me too.

Is it any wonder that I have struggled with this thing called love for all of my life and that, for me, it has been that which I have most sought after?

You will probably think me biased when I tell you that upon discovering the Bible, I seized upon the love of God for us as my life raft. You could say, of course, what else would he see in the Bible? Okay, I plead guilty as charged, and if I were the only one ever to read, "For God so loved the world that He gave his one and only son, that whoever believes in him shall not perish but have eternal life" (John 3:16), I would certainly be biased by my upbringing. Yes, I have struggled with love, but I found that the phrase "Love is a decision" to be true, and with time and especially with the help of my wife Sue (I call her Suzie), who had her own flawed childhood, we are discovering love one step at a time.

Look for flaws in my reasoning, if you will, as I lay out my claim that the Bible is only about God's love for his children, and that we are only in this world to learn to love as he loves us.

Let's start with the great commandment. Jesus was tested by the Sadducees, and he won. Then the Pharisees tried their hand at catching Jesus in some kind of scriptural error. So they asked him to give his opinion on which was the greatest commandment of the Law (the first five books of the Old Testament). Jesus answers with:

> Love the Lord your God with all your heart, and with all your soul, and with all your mind. This is the first and greatest commandment. And the second is like it. Love your neighbor as yourself. All the law and the prophets hang on these two commandments. (Matt 22:32–40)

The first and greatest is a quote from Deuteronomy 6:4, and the second from Leviticus 19:18—both books of the Mosaic law. So Jesus upholds the law and tells them and us what God most wants us to know about life.

These priests and scribes were most interested in preserving their status, but Jesus was talking of how we should all live.

The Bible is talking to us, so let us delve deeper and listen more. If I am right in my quest to show the Bible only as a book of God's love for us and his desire that we should love as he loves us, then let's look to Jesus's only direct commandment to us as a place to go next. In John 13:34–35, he says, "A new commandment I give you. Love one another. As I have loved you, so you must love one another. By this all men will know that you are my disciples, if you love one another."

This commandment and challenge are too big for me if I am on my own. I know the selfishness and self-centeredness that lives in me, and I know I am not the only one. Jesus offers me a carrot on a stick or, better yet, the brass ring of all rings—the kingdom of heaven. It is a frightening yet awesomely wonderful offer: "Those who find their life will lose it, and those who lose their life for my sake will find it" (Matthew 10:39).

The parable of the pearl of great price is one of the ways in which he tells us of the value of our choice. Jesus continues with the parable of the net being cast for fish, which are then separated into good and bad, with the bad being cast away. This passage is completed by connecting these parables to the kingdom. "Therefore, every teacher of the law who has been instructed about the kingdom of heaven is like the owner of a house who brings out of his storeroom new treasures as well as old" (Matthew 13:52). We must find the treasure and the pearl, and we do this by leaning on Jesus in us to practice his love.

As I consider this, I am drawn to the words of Jesus in the Gospel of John speaking of himself being the vine and us the branches. He says…

> Abide in me as I abide in you. Just as the branch cannot bear fruit by itself unless it abides in the vine, neither can you unless you abide in me. I am the vine; you are the branches. Those who abide in me and I in them bear much fruit, because apart from me you can do nothing. Whoever does not abide in me is thrown away like a branch and withers; such branches are gathered, thrown into the fire, and burned. (John 15:4–6)

CHAPTER 2

WHY THE NEED FOR KINGDOM EYES?

MY THEOLOGICAL BASE

Theology comes to us on many levels, and I got the scholarly things in college with my BS degree in religion from Texas Wesleyan University, and then in seminary with my master of divinity degree from Brite Divinity School at Texas Christian University. It is said that higher education just gives you the tools to know where to look for the answers you need and the kinds of questions to ask. That was certainly true for me.

What I learned in my formal education has given me the skeleton on which to build my faith. I draw on my education all of the time, but it is my experiences with God along the way that, more than anything else, have shaped how I read the Bible. I do believe that John Wesley had it right when he said that the tradition of the church, reason, and experience are ways that we can come to understand God in our lives. Yet, as he said, these only work with the Bible firmly at the center of our journey of faith.

I lean heavily on my experience with God through the Holy Spirit in understanding the good news as it appears in the Bible. The Bible, and especially the good news that Jesus brings to us all, is at the center of my faith, and as I walk through this world and read his Word, he teaches me how to walk in the kingdom now.

My education informs me of tradition, my reason helps me to integrate all of the input a faith walk brings, and my experiences with God through prayer, vision, and walking the walk make the Bible come alive for me.

However, we may try to understand the Bible in the same way someone might try to understand how a shovel works by grabbing it from the blade end and poking the handle at the ground. We take our worldly understanding of life and of people and their emotions, and then look to God to try and put it all into perspective. In his book, *Your God Is Too Small,* J. B. Phillips tells us that even if you take the best person you have ever met—the noblest, most honorable, and loving person—and multiply that person by a million, you would not begin to grasp who God is.

What we have to do is to let God into our lives and let him change us from within. We will not necessarily understand him better intellectually, but our hearts will be closer to him at a deep level, and we will have a better grasp of who he is.

There is a joke about a man climbing up a dangerous mountain to ask the guru at the top, "What is the meaning of life?" The answers this joke gives in its many forms vary, but one on them is "Life is a head of cabbage." (This is where you are expected to laugh out of confusion.)

My defining answers come as I climb the mountain spiritually. God needs us as much as we need him, and the answer to how to approach him is found in loving others. Those are the foundational answers for my faith walk.

Perhaps the best place to begin to find answers is with the question "who are we?" I believe that we are eternal beings created by God to live with him forever if we choose. How shall we get to do this? By believing in the name of Jesus and by living under grace—not by rules or by trying to live a "good moral life" because we cannot do that. We cannot always be good enough, but under grace, the Spirit will guide us into right actions and bring us back to the path when we go astray.

At some point in eternity, God called us into his mind (an oxymoron, for is there such a thing as a point in eternity where time is relevant?), and then placed us by birth into this world. We United Methodists believe in prevenient grace—that he is always speaking to us and opening doors for us to discover and rediscover him and that we are offered knowledge of him. How we respond to him reaching out to us determines where we will dwell in eternity.

So God is forever, and somewhere in eternity, he decided to create what we call the universe and to place us in a very small arm of it. The point is that in our sojourn here, we could return his love by learning to love ourselves and others as "he has loved us."

God is the alpha and omega, the beginning and the end. He knew the fall would happen and was already planning the coming of the Christ. So he carved out a place where time is relevant—at least it is to us. He put us here in this place, and even though our eternal nature is as spirits in his image, we get caught up in the physical. This is a condition that John calls walking around in darkness.

"This is the verdict, Light has come into the world, but men loved darkness instead of light because their deeds were evil" (John 3:19).

"I have come into the world as a light, so that no one who believes in me should stay in darkness" (John 12:46).

Most of us have been raised with an idea that sin is something you do, but Jesus wants us to know that evil is as deep as our spirits go. Evil springs from our desire for self-preservation, which then leads to us trying to control the world we live in so that things go our way. This is the evil—selfishness and self-centeredness—that lives in us.

Yes, some of us seem to enter this world with a kind and giving spirit, but this is not true for most of us. We have to be taught by trial and error (and by the spirit of God) how to give as much or more than we receive and then how to do so gladly.

Here is a mystery that God alone can fully understand. God, who was there in the beginning, is already there at the end. He has already seen every event of our lives and all of those before us and all of those to come after us. We get to make our choices (hopefully letting the Holy Spirit guide us), but God who is in eternity sees it all as one huge movie. After all, he is the God of creation, the God of history, and he is in control of it all.

Some will say that he has done a bad job, considering all of the evil that takes place in this world. However, that evil is in us, and he is calling all of us who will listen out of this world. The world can then be seen as a proving ground of souls. We get to walk in the darkness until we get tired of it and look toward Him. He is already there opening doors for us to perceive him, and he is ready to lead us into eternity.

We are eternal spiritual beings, created in the image of God who is *the eternal spiritual being*. In Old Testament times, the spirit of God came to certain people (mostly prophets) on special occasions, but was not always there. However, Jeremiah foretold of the time that this would change:

> "This is the covenant I will make with the house of Israel after that time," declares the Lord. "I will put my law in their minds and write it on their hearts. I will be their God, and they will be my people." (Jeremiah 31:33)

This is the in-dwelling of the Spirit that was to come with the Messiah whom Jeremiah and Isaiah predicted (Isaiah 42:3 and Isaiah 53:1–12)

In the New Testament, Jesus proclaims that God and he will make their home in us (John 14:23), and the Holy Spirit will be sent by God in Jesus's name and "will teach you all things."

So we should know that, as spirits in the image of God, everything we do, think, and feel is a spiritual event and known to God. This spirit of God is with us to teach us how to love as Jesus loves us (John 13). That is the path to the kingdom of God.

John 15 is a chapter about relationships where Jesus again tells his disciples to love each other, but it is also where he says that he is the true vine and that they cannot bear good fruit unless they stay in him as he is in them.

Then he says that he no longer calls them servants but friends, and that he is sending the advocate "whom I will send you from the Father, even the Spirit of truth…he will testify about me, and you must also testify, for you have been with me from the beginning."

John 14 is where Jesus tells his disciples that "in my Father's house there are many rooms" and that he is preparing a place there for them. This is the kingdom of heaven that is mentioned 158 times in the New Testament. This is the goal of every Christian, but the way there is clearly through the heart.

Then, as Matthew reminds us, of all the things in this world that we feel we need, we must "seek first His kingdom and His righteousness, and all these things will be given to you as well" (Matthew 6:33).

So what is "righteousness?" Webster says that it is "acting in accord with divine or moral law: free from guilt or sin." He adds that it is a "morally right or justifiable (a *righteous)* decision."

Second Samuel 22:25 says, "The Lord has rewarded me according to my righteousness, according to my cleanness in his sight" and Psalm 24:3–4 adds:

> Who may ascend the hill of the Lord?
> Who may stand in his holy place?
> He who has clean hands and a pure heart.
> Who does not lift up his soul to an idol or swear by what is false;
> He will receive blessing from the Lord and vindication from
> God his Savior.

So we can see that a person with clean hands is one who acts justly toward all. He or she is a person with deep love for God and for his children and always works for the good of others as much or more so than his self. This is the path to the kingdom of heaven and to brotherhood with Christ.

That God needs us as much as we need him explains for me his actions in Jesus's having been born of a woman. He could have said he loves us in a myriad of ways, and yet he chose to walk among us and experienced life as we do. Christ is only our Savior if he is fully human and can feel our questions and our doubts. If Jesus the man can't feel the evil that works in and around me and all of us in this world in a very personal way, then the God in him has come for no purpose at all. The man Jesus also needs to feel adoration of God from our point of view to know all the ways we feel about him, and thus have a true empathy with us.

We can get a glimpse of how it might feel for God to lose his control over all things by reading John Howard Griffin's book *Black Like Me.* A white man with his privileges over Blacks in 1960s

America gets to experience having little or no control over his life as he travels through the southern United States as a Black man.

Jesus, who is one with God in the Holy Trinity, is also fully a man. He enters into the world of his people as one of them. The difference between him and Griffin is that Jesus came not to observe and tell all to bring about change but to change the world from within.

My God needs me to love him as much as he loves me, and He does everything needed to get our attention and to show us his love. He showed us his hands and asks us to show him ours. And the biggest problem we have with that is that we can't see the God who is in us, so we dismiss his call for us to love as he does as being beyond our ability. Our humanness becomes our excuse. Yet Jesus says in John 14:23 that "Anyone who loves me will obey my teaching. My Father will love them, and we will come to them and make our home with them."

In 1 John 4:20, we read, "Whoever claims to love God, but hates a brother or sister is a liar. For whoever does not love their brother and sister, whom they have seen, cannot love God, whom they have not seen."

All of us may not actively hate someone else, but most of us harbor grudges and dislikes that block us from loving others. So the call to love like God becomes our stumbling block.

I recognize that, for myself, part of my not being able to love for most of my life had to do with my very effective defenses. Others couldn't hurt my feelings, so I didn't have to hate them. I could just dismiss them. Of course, those ample defenses of mine also kept out those I could have loved. I didn't have to hate you, but neither could I love you.

I would have had to risk dropping my defenses and let myself be hurt in order to hate or to love. The problem with loving others is that we have to be vulnerable to the slings and arrows of others toward us as much as to the love of others for us. To us humans, this goes against what we believe is possible, and so we shut off God's will for us at that point.

Making God's call to us a lesser thing also makes God less personal, for it is his love and desire for a deeply personal relationship with us that is at the center of all that is.

I have read the parable of the pearl of great price a number of times, but as I have read it in recent years, I have come to feel "the fear and trembling" Paul talks of as he speaks of us working out our salvation. God is calling me to die as the Jim Van Rite I know, to give up being me and become Jim Van Rite, personal friend of God. He wants me to walk in his likeness for all to see.

Recently, I was meditating in a half-awake state in the morning, and this thought came to me: *At my best as a human, people just see me. But, as I surrender to God, people begin to see a little of God in me. The further I get in my faith journey others should see more of God and less of me.* I look forward to this journey.

I believe all of us are called to this high calling. But who will hear and actually listen so as to act out this calling?

Jesus quotes Isaiah:

> With them indeed is fulfilled the prophecy of Isaiah that says: "You will indeed listen, but never understand, and you will indeed look, but never perceive. For this people's heart has grown dull, and their ears are hard of hearing, and they have shut their eyes, so that they might not look with their eyes, and listen with their ears, and understand with their heart and turn—and I would heal them." (Matthew 13:15)

Like many others, I have run from the words of Jesus when they are too hard and scare me. And when I run, the words above aptly describe me. My heart becomes dull and lifeless, my faith walk slows to a crawl (if not a dead stop) because I can't see the road ahead. But this happens only because the change he wants in me is scaring and confusing me.

Just a few years ago, I was at this point for the umpteenth time. I felt God calling me to a closer walk, but as so many times in the past, I was seeing this closer walk as a loss rather than a gain. How much of my life was I willing to put aside or risk losing in order to gain what he was offering? I came to the conclusion that whatever the cost, I would risk it for the gain that I knew deep in my heart was there.

Suzie and I have a lifestyle that centers around our church and the people who attend it, our best friends, and of course, our children and grandchildren. We bought a house several years ago, and a large part of our money has gone into remodeling it and to making it our own.

At the same time, since I was raised in Aruba for much of my life, we went there a couple of years ago with our good friends. Now we have a casual dream of living in the Caribbean. That scenario, and one of much travel, would mean focusing our future entirely on ourselves. So letting God dictate our future instead would easily be seen as a loss.

The cost of letting God redefine our future needs to be one of seeing the gain in it, and we are trying to do that. A trip to Scotland and northern England to worship with a modern group who model their faith on the example of ancient Celtic Christians was a way to begin. (More on this later.)

SCIENCE AND REALITY

Plato believed that our senses couldn't be trusted as they are activated by the mortal body and not by the immortal soul. Therefore, the reality we sense will not sustain us on a journey toward finding the real.

Only a very few will be able to be aware, through intellect, of the perfect place of forms—the timeless place. If some do grasp this higher plane intellectually, they almost surely will not be able to convince others that they have seen it and that it is what is truly real. His allegory of the prisoners in a cave sitting around a fire is one of his explanations. If someone were to escape the cave where only shadows were seen, and then try to return to free others, they would not be able to convince any others to leave the cave with them.

Plato's work is close to being what is known as Gnosticism, which is salvation through knowledge. I have come to see reality in the light of Jesus who lived in the kingdom now and in the world at the same time. We, on the other hand, live in this world, and as John put it in John 3:19–21:

> This is the verdict: Light has come into the world, but people loved darkness instead of light because their deeds were evil. Everyone who does evil hates the light for fear that their deeds will be exposed. But whoever lives by the truth comes into the light, so that it may be seen plainly that what they have done has been done in the sight of God.

The light and the darkness are two different realities. Someone living in darkness cannot see the light, while someone living in the light knows of the darkness but chooses the light where truth is apparent.

The line drawn by John is not as clear in this world where few, if any of us, ever live fully in the light while we are alive. Christians, as much as others, are caught up in the darkness of the drama of life, and getting free so as to know the truth requires that we be willing to die to self so the new self can begin to learn how to live in the light step by step.

Our reality is what we expect it to be, so if we are glass-half-empty people, we expect bad to happen. Glass-half-full people expect more good than bad to happen, but few Christians expect that they can ever be free enough to love as Christ commanded. And because we find that so hard to imagine, we are like the prisoners in Plato's cave. For the most part, we don't expect to get into the kingdom now so fully as to live from God's point of view. If we would commit more fully to the death of our own will, we would live more fully in the kingdom than in this world, and our reality would change.

You could say that we would be living in the real world—the eternal world—as opposed to the darkness, which is not eternal and, because of its opposition to the light, will not survive.

If you read anything about the current discussions going on in the world of physics, you will probably find discussions about such things as, Is time real, or do we really live in a three-dimensional world? The answers many persons give are (1) no, there is no such thing as time as we experience it, and (2) we are living in a giant hologram that gives the illusion of three dimensions.

These seem like answers to questions that we never ask, and in fact, most non-physicists never have and never will ask such questions. I only bring these physics oddities up to discuss the kingdom of God and what we call the real world.

If our thinking process is God-centric where we see God as everywhere and in everything, or just that the kingdom of God is all around us and even in us, then it is easy to see God and the kingdom as real and this world as an illusion. Clearly, it is right to say that we'll never get out of this world alive, so at best this world is temporary, and the eternity that is God and the kingdom are a forever that existed before this world and will exist afterward. Given that the kingdom is forever, then a universe that has lasted billions and billions of years is still less than an eye-blink by comparison. So which is ultimately real?

If, as I believe from my own God-centric point of view, that God created this world so as to bring us into being and then into fellowship as his children, and that, as his children we are only here to learn to love God and others as He loves us, then this world is just a kindergarten, a pseudo-reality carved out by God to train us to be family members forever.

Farfetched? Not any more so than what those modern physicists believe, for they could be right, and it wouldn't matter for God's creation. God still intends, above all else, to draw as many of us as will to come into the kingdom which is still now and forever. He wants his family with him, and we are that family.

In Acts 12:24–28, Paul says to the Athenians:

> The God who made the world and everything in it is Lord of Heaven and earth…he gives everyone life and breath and everything else… God did this so they would see him and perhaps reach out for him and find him, though he is not far from any of us. For in him we live and move and have our being. As some of your own poets have said, "we are his offspring."

Consider Jesus, whom we believe was both divine and human while on earth. Fathered by God and born of a woman, he lived in the eternal kingdom and in this world at the same time. To him, the water at the wedding in Cana could be either water, wine, or anything else, for in the eternal kingdom, the rules that govern the universe as we perceive it don't exist.

Therefore, Jesus can say to the disciples that with the faith of a mustard seed they could say to a bush, "Go, be planted in the sea, or move a mountain somewhere else."

WHO IS GOD? AND WHO AM I?

I would like to visit two most important issues about our Creator and about us as his created beings.

First, the most powerful concept in any language comes from the verb *to be*. God answers Moses question as to his name by saying, "Thus you shall say to the Israelites, I am has sent me to you" (Exodus 3:14).

"I am" is not a name. It is an ultimate statement of God's assuredness of his existence and his place in the scheme of all things. Here, it is an action statement, inferring that in fact God is the creator of all. "I am" here in Exodus is also an ultimate statement about God's *beingness*, i.e., God is the ultimate being, and all things begin with or come from him.

Jesus teases us with what it might feel like to be a little like God by saying, "If you have faith the size of this mustard seed, you will say to this mountain, 'Move from here to here,' and it will move; and nothing will be impossible for you" (Matthew 17:20).

The power to create or to move mountains is something humans do not have but can be given through faith. It is a question of who *am I*, and *where do I belong*? If I can't see or feel God in me, then I can't see what he can do in me or, at least, in some of his children.

An earthly model of what assuredness of self can bring is seen in people with a strong sense of self. I will argue that only someone with some of God's goodness in him or her can truly be a strong self.

Even Satan has the weakness of knowing he is less than God and is envious even in full fight mode.

So someone with a strong sense of self is easily seen for this trait by others. I am not saying that they will act out of love in all situations—they may act badly at times—but by knowing the strength of their effect on others, many will eventually learn to modify their behavior so as to be more of a positive force than a negative one.

It is not necessarily true that a strong sense of self equates to a secure sense of self. Someone with a powerful personality to command others by the force of their words and strength of presence may at the same time have their feelings hurt quite easily. It is not hard to find world leaders or industry tycoons who, for all their commanding presence, do not handle criticism very well.

Second, this brings me to how we identify ourselves as a "self" and why that can make us vulnerable to the words and presence of other-selves.

Richard Rohr, a Catholic priest, writer, and lecturer, is one of many to have taken on the task of outlining a list of steps for spiritual growth. He says that in the first three steps, we move from our body image of who we are to our external actions, and then to our thoughts and feelings to try and grasp who we are and how we fit into this world.

It is only then that we can look deeper and plumb those deeper thoughts and feelings of selfhood. Before step 4, we compare ourselves to others. At step 4, we are comparing ourselves to the internal word of God, whom we are only then beginning to feel.

Rohr and others who teach spiritual growth tell us that most of us will shy away from God at the point of meeting him—whatever they call that step.

The great "I am" is ultimate self, and we feel our tininess before him and compare ourselves to him. It is a scary thing to face the ultimate being, and most of us run from him when we get this far because what is ahead is the road to what we call sanctification. And if we don't find that scary, then we haven't really heard his call.

In my own journey, I reached a point where I grew weary of having to apologize to God again and again for falling short in my attempts to love my neighbor as myself. So, when Suzie and I switched our church membership to Martin United Methodist Church in Bedford, I saw this as a good time to risk growing spiritually, which meant for me to risk being open and vulnerable to others. It meant letting the Holy Spirit guide me into more often risking loving actions toward others. Accepting a position as associate pastor at Martin put me squarely into the middle of that opportunity to grow in love for others. I went to God in prayer and admitted that I was fearful of letting him tear down my emotional defenses against being vulnerable to others. The key to getting the help I was needing was for me to step out and do loving actions toward others. I was now being present for them. People need to feel heard if they are to believe that they are valued, and I set out to listen better than I had been doing in the past.

When I retired from Martin UMC, there was an amazing amount of love shown to Suzie and me by the church members. I had made progress in being *with* people spiritually; and Suzie—well, she is just lovable by nature!

All who call themselves Christians have encountered enough of God to believe in him. Most just don't stay there in his presence long enough to let him lead them deeper into fellowship with him. Grace is sufficient to save all who "believe in his name" (John 1:12), but we cheat ourselves and others by not letting the Holy Spirit guide us from salvation into sanctification.

Therefore, I believe that anyone who has not encountered God and stood in there with him can be an authentically strong self, as the strong self understands that it is only by being humble before God that we find our strongest beingness.

In the prologue to John's gospel, we hear that the word, which was with God always, was the one through whom all things were created. Then John repeats that by saying, "without him not one thing came into being" (John 1:3). Next John says, "In him was life, and the life was the light to all people. The light shines in the darkness and the darkness did not overcome it" (John 1:4–5). Combine these verses with John 3:16 where Jesus says, "He gave his only son, so that everyone who believes in him may not perish but have eternal life."

Here we can grasp, if we will, what God is doing in us. He made us into beings who can respond to him in spirit because his life force/Spirit is in us and is a light in the darkness of the world—a light that will guide us to him if we let it do so. The eternal life he offers is a personal relationship for now as well as forever. This is the fearsome part that only a few (whom we recognize as saints, as Paul speaks of them in Philippians 2:12–13) have chosen to risk. It is indeed "fearsome" to enter into such a relationship with the ultimate self. The change in our small selves that is required is like a seismic shift of the continents on the earth's mantle. Luckily, this is not expected all at once, but the journey into sanctification is nevertheless a journey into the ultimate. Is there any wonder that Proverbs 9:10 tells us that, "The fear of the Lord is the beginning of wisdom, and the knowledge of the Holy One is insight."

So there are strong selves compared to others, and there are strong selves because of staying in the presence of God.

Jesus says, "I am the resurrection and the life. Those who believe in me, even though they die, will live" (John 11:25). In seven other "I am" statements, he is showing the power of knowing who he is. Just as with the Father's use of these words, it is all about ultimate creative and protective power within the Trinity.

So I often say, "God is, therefore we are." We are created by him for him to be like him if we choose.

In another place, I speak of how at a soul level we are offered guidance by the Holy Spirit and at the same time buffeted by the evil spirit of Satan.

Meditating at four this morning, I thought of the pool of "Beth-zatha" where a blind and lame man waited to be put in the disturbed water and be healed (John 5:2–9).

God has disturbed my peace at the level of my soul over most of my life, and it took me many years to see that this was about healing my "self" and my poor self-esteem. He has been leading me toward a healthy sense of self. Whether or not I ever reach the faith of a mustard seed, I do know that I am on the way by the grace of God.

THE KINGDOM OF GOD

There is a chasm between us humans and God—one that Jesus came to fix. The chasm is between the ultimate nature of God (and his perfection) and Jesus's call for us to be perfect also. That hardly seems like a fix to us.

As I was finishing seminary, I began to see the chasm as more of an illusion than as a fact. What we see as two different realities only appears that way because we cling to the world too tightly for the Holy Spirit to show us both at once.

The kingdom of God, as Jesus offers it, is a place of infinite possibilities for us—God's children. However, this world's values and the scientific underpinnings on which our modern society runs are faulty in the extreme.

The Apostle Paul had a high-level education and a good grasp of the world of his time, and yet he said in Philippians 3:7–10 (New Revised Standard Version, Anglicized [NRSVA]):

> Yet whatever gains I had, these I have come to regard as loss because of Christ. More than that, I regard everything as loss because of the surpassing value of knowing Christ Jesus my Lord. For his sake I have suffered the loss of all things, and I regard them as rubbish, in order that I may gain Christ and be found in him, not having a righteousness of my own that comes from the law, but one that comes through faith in Christ, the righteousness from God based on faith. I want to know Christ and the power of his resurrection and the sharing of his sufferings by becoming like him in his death.

What is this kingdom about which Jesus tells in the parables of the treasure in a field and the pearl of great price?

Everything we believe to be true and right based on our knowledge of the world is worthless because of the basic premises with which the world starts us. The world teaches that in general we are basically good. Evil exists, but hope springs eternal for those who believe that the world will overcome its destructive self, and humans will rise up and exceed our past. Most of what is taught about the kingdom of God is flawed because of an equally bad starting premise. Most people, including most Christians, assume that perfection is so far out of our reach that we should settle for what is good in this world and not for the wonders of the kingdom now. We will be rewarded in the kingdom to come for being good or for being faithful now. Being faithful now is a good thing, but if our understanding stops there, we will miss out on so much of what God offers us.

Jesus lived, taught, worked miracles, died, and was resurrected to teach us that we can have the wonders of the kingdom now. So much of what he teaches in the gospels flies in the face of what we believe is possible, and that is the reason that we are not in touch with our spirits and our souls. The result is that we don't realize the eternal power of what we feel, say, and do.

When we belittle someone, that hurt forever reverberates through our own spirits, the one we hurt, and others. And it adds to the negative vibes of a fallen world. We add to the misery of the whole world through casual pettiness and intended harm that we dish out.

When we act out of love, the opposite occurs. We add to the momentum toward the kingdom now. It shouldn't be hard to see that if we could wrap our understanding of reality around these two possibilities—the eternal reverberations of the good and evil we cause—we would not find perfection and the kingdom now to be so impossible.

We are each very tiny in the grand scheme of the kingdom's coming because of Christ, but when all human interactions are counted, those billions and billions of interactions over all of the lifetimes ever lived and those that are now being lived add up to the engine that drives human good and evil. The Holy Spirit intervenes, but we still have free will. God intervened in Christ, or there would be no hope. And all of the goodness done in this world is because the Holy Spirit enters into all of the lives ever lived to open us to doing love. But it is up to us to choose to do so.

I had a vision of God standing in the wind of all human thoughts, emotions, and actions, and smelling the aroma of each individual, whether pleasing to him or not, and knowing each one to the core of their being. God alone can survive the onslaught of all this human input.

> As a pleasing odor I will accept you, when I bring you out from the peoples, and gather you out of the countries where you have been scattered; and I will manifest my holiness among you in the sight of the nations. You shall know that I am the Lord, when I bring you into the land of Israel, the country that I swore to give to your ancestors. There you shall remember your ways and all the deeds by which you have polluted yourselves; and you shall loathe yourselves for all the evils that you have committed. And you shall know that I am the Lord, when I deal with you for my name's sake, not according to your evil ways, or corrupt deeds, O house of Israel, says the Lord God. (Ezekiel 20:41–44)

God speaks to the aroma of his creatures in places other than Ezekiel as a way of describing one of the ways we are known to him. As I dreamed the above dream or had the vision (which ever it was), I also realized that this world was created for humankind alone. He gave us dominion over all created things and set the table for us to be joined with him eternally as the family of God. The world would perish in what we know as time, for it is only our classroom. The choice between good and evil is necessary for us to learn what it means to be like him.

The kingdom of God is eternal. This world is not. It is God's intention to conform this world to the kingdom, and the Lord's Prayer asks us to pray for that to happen.

The gospel of Jesus Christ is about the kingdom now as it is in heaven. This is God's aim for us all. His aim is for nothing less than the total redemption of the whole world. He wants all who will to come to him and to be full members of the household of God. His want for us, as the old hymn ("What a Friend We Have in Jesus") says, is for us "to carry everything to God in prayer." He wants to carry our sins and griefs.

He wants us to try and live up to his love now. He wants to guide us in this endeavor, and he wants to show us the narrow road and its rewards. The problem is that for us to even grasp what the rewards of the narrow road are, we need to use our *kingdom eyes*. Then we will feel a different kind of pleasure than the world has for us. Love like God's kind of love reshapes our whole being and deeply enriches our soul talk so that we can look upon others as the beloved of God and try to treat them accordingly. The reward of kingdom sight and kingdom living is then a kind of pleasure that those living only in this world cannot imagine and those who are attempting to live in the kingdom-now will find scary and yet exciting. Sometimes the hymns we sing in holy worship give us warmth in our hearts that we can appreciate as heavenly as compared to worldly. We don't have to be able to explain it, but for that moment in time, we can feel the rewards of the kingdom.

The parable of the mustard seed spoke to me as a real challenge. I began to grasp the understanding that the kingdom of God on earth was all around me, and that it was the lenses that I was looking through that kept me from seeing it.

My lenses were shaped by the reality that I thought this world to be. By this I mean this stuff we have and see—the natural world around us and our relationships with all of their drama. This is real, isn't it? The Lord's Prayer given by Jesus says:

> Thy kingdom come,
> Thy will be done
> On earth as it is in heaven.

On earth as it is in heaven? Is Jesus asking us to live in heavenly/kingdom ways now? Is he asking us to make the imperatives he called us to— such as being perfect as our heavenly Father is perfect, forgiving as God does, or loving each other as he loves us— real in our lives?

I am convinced that it is. In Psalm 82:6, we hear "you are gods, you are all sons of the most high." Then Jesus quotes this psalm in John 10:34: "is it not written in your law, 'I have said you are gods.'

If he called them 'gods,' to whom the word of God came—and Scripture cannot be set aside—what about the one whom the Father set apart as his very own and sent into the world?"

Jesus had been accused of blasphemy for calling himself God's son, and he is saying we are gods and sons of God, if we hear and obey and understand our calling. What I am leading to by quoting Jesus, from the Gospel of John, is that the kingdom of God now and the kingdom of God realized are the same. Jesus brought the kingdom now into this world by being born, and during his ministry here, he showed us how the kingdom is supposed to be here and now as well as then. Again "on earth as it is in heaven."

Jesus brought the kingdom now with him and lived in it and the world at the same time. He offered us the same options, and even said that if we had the faith of a mustard seed, then we could move a bush or a mountain to other places, or that we could work greater signs than he did. Why would he say that if he didn't mean it?

Now, I am not suggesting that we should all try to work miracles willy-nilly. The narrow road into the kingdom is a road paved by you and me doing acts of love without regard to what we get in return.

The "pearl of great price" that Jesus told about in a parable was something the merchant sought more than all others that he had. And so he sold all he had in order to get it.

Recently, I preached a sermon in which I said that it is like you and me encountering this pearl of greatest wonder and realizing we could have it if we gave up all that we have in this world—our material possessions, money, and relationships now and hoped for—and offered all of this to God for this perfect pearl. I asked, "Could you make this trade? Could I?" I said that if we see the trade as a loss, then we value what we have and hope for in this world as of more value than what God has to offer.

KINGDOM EYES

On the other hand, if we see it as a gain, then we receive a new point of view, which I call kingdom eyes. Kingdom eyes is about how we are called to be changed into active members of the family of God, showing the world that God is even now working through us to defeat evil one person at a time.

If the pearl of great price is not even on our radar, then this discussion is moot. So say we have a glimmer of something God has for us, and the wonder of it is just beyond our ability to focus on, then this is when we open ourselves to the Holy Spirit calling us into the family circle.

The early church had many growing pains on the way to the established understanding of the Trinity and Christian lifestyle that are at the mainstream of today's church, and some of the hardest of these growing pains to deal with are still with us today.

Shall we renounce most of our earthly pleasures as sinful (or that at the very least they lead us into sin), or shall we look upon the material lifestyle as no problem for a life of faith in Jesus Christ? Is there a viable in-between position, or is there another completely different way of looking at how a Christian (which can mean "little Christ") should live.

Consider Revelation 2:6: "You have this in your favor; you hate the practice of the Nicolaitans, which I also hate." The Nicolaitans based their authority on their leader, Nicolaus. Since Nicolaus was ordained by the apostles as a deacon, his followers believed that they had authority from the apostles. They followed their leaders without question. They believed in finding knowledge through complete unrestraint. Sexual immorality was their primary focus. They claimed that sins committed in the body did not affect the spirit (Wikipedia 2021).

On the opposite side were those who would have Christians live a totally ascetic lifestyle, turning their back on the world. Allowing the Holy Spirit to lead us into grace is the key here.

Consider Matthew 6:31–34: "so do worry saying, 'what shall we eat or what shall we drink? or what shall we wear? For the pagans run after all these things, and your heavenly Father knows that you need them. *But seek first his kingdom and his righteousness, and all these things will be given to you as well.* Therefore, do not worry about tomorrow for tomorrow will worry about itself. Each day has enough trouble of its own" (emphasis mine).

The fruits of the spirit give us an outline of what our lives should look and feel like, and in pursuing a life under grace, we will not need any laws but God's law of love to govern our behavior. True, God's law of love will not substitute for highway speed laws and such, but our lives will be otherwise led by the Holy Spirit and exemplary in so far as our relations with God and others are concerned.

So we should ask the Spirit to help us to seek the kingdom by living our lives within God's will, and by his law of loving him and others as much as ourselves.

That is the spiritual lifestyle. That is living in the Spirit. The result will be that, as we try on this lifestyle and move further into it, we will acquire a lifestyle in which the career path that we are on and the things that we obtain along the way do not dominate our lives; rather, they will be the result of seeking the kingdom first. This is what I call having kingdom eyes.

Here again, we step onto the narrow road by doing acts of love, as John Wesley suggested: "Do all the good you can; By all the means you can, In all the ways you can; In all the places you can; At all the times you can; To all the people you can; As long as ever you can."

The second emphasis in Wesley's understanding of salvation is also hinted at in the definition above. When salvation is focused on forgiveness and "going to heaven," it takes on strong individualistic tones since these are usually seen as discreet events for each person. By contrast, Wesley insisted that salvation was fundamentally social in nature. In the words of his well-known aphorism: "there is no holiness but social holiness."

For John Wesley, salvation is inextricably linked with faith. If the end of the Christian religion is salvation, the "means to attain it [is] faith" (SW 43). In its broadest sense, Wesley describes faith as a new way of seeing. It is a mode of sight by which people may perceive the previously unseen spiritual world and become convinced of God and his work (SW 46–47). He notes that Scripture refers to faith as "light exhibited to the soul, and a supernatural sight or perception thereof" (SW 46). It is both a new faculty of vision and light for the exercise of that faculty.

According to John Wesley, the goal of genuine Christian religion may be summarized in one word: *salvation.* See his works *The Scripture Way of Salvation* and *A Plain Account of Christian Perfection.*

Living out our salvation is an everyday way of doing loving things which will warm and change our hearts and help us to see what we were blind to before. Somewhere along the narrow road that will open before us because of this way of living, we will begin to see that pearl of great price that is before us, and with our warmed and opened hearts, a step at a time, we will begin making the trade of our worldly things and viewpoints for what God wants us to have.

Everyone is different, and our path to the narrow road, and even the shape of the part of the road we are on, will be different, for all of us have our own wagon load of stuff to recognize as detrimental and to turn it loose. Will God keep it all, leaving us in poverty? Maybe for a few of us, but most likely he will just show us how to prioritize our belongings so that he always comes first in our lives. In Matthew 6:31–34, we read:

> So do not worry, saying, what shall we eat? Or What shall we drink? Or What shall we wear? For the pagans run after all these things, and your heavenly Father knows that you need them. But seek first his Kingdom and his righteousness, and all these things will be given to you.

CHAPTER 3

THE BIBLE AND KINGDOM EYES

THE BIBLE AS CONVERSATION WITH GOD

This is another of my early-morning meditations with God.

First there came the thought that *the Bible is a conversation with God,* then later these words flowed from my fingertips to my computer. No, I was no auto-writer, but the words did flow freely from my fingertips. There was, of course, my thought process involved, because I had to bring up from memory the place where God spoke to his people in the Old Testament and from the New Testament. There are many more that I could cite and still more that I have either forgotten or of which I am unaware. I seek to have kingdom eyes and a kingdom heart, and these conversations that I have with God early in the morning are some of the ways he is teaching me.

The Bible is a conversation between God and his creation. He begins by speaking creation into existence, and if you listen to John 1:1–18, the Word of God that was heard speaking in creation was he who was born of Mary: Jesus. As John writes in the gospel, he was there "in the beginning with God. All things came into being through him, and without him, not one thing came into being."

He spoke Adam and Eve into existence along with the earth and all that is in it. This is true, even if you believe solely in evolution, since the garden story works just as well as a creation myth that tells of how the God who created everything wants a relationship with us and about what happened when they ate of the tree of the knowledge of good and evil. He gave them plenty to eat but without the knowledge of good and evil. So God's kind (humans) couldn't converse with him any more than a dog or cat can converse with us in an intelligent way.

After they ate of the tree of knowledge of good and evil, God said to himself as Father, Son, and Holy Spirit, "See, the man has become like one of us, knowing good and evil; and now he might reach out his hand and take also from the tree of life and eat of it and live forever"(Genesis 3:22). Perhaps he was also speaking to the angels of heaven.

But the point is clear: humans, made from God himself, now had the capacity to choose him out of a rudimentary understanding of who and what God is. We could know ourselves as spirits made of the stuff of God and thus know him as our Creator in a much more personal way than Adam and Eve could have at first. In any case, we can let Eve off the hook as God got what he wanted—people with a spirit made after his own whom he could invite into his family forever. All they had to do and all we have to do is to accept it.

Did humans born through evolution always have this sense of a relationship with God, or did God not at some point breathe himself into humans so that they would have his spirit within themselves?

Whether you accept the Genesis story at face value or not, evolution did not produce a soul (a spirit) like that of God. God wanted us as his own, and at some point, he entered into us in such a way as to make that possible. Whether in the Garden of Eden or in evolution or both, one thing we who have felt him calling from within us know is that he is here. He is in us, and we can feel his presence. And we feel it because he talks to us first, and he wants to draw us near to him within the depths of ourselves. And, because of this opening us to himself, we can become God's friends.

So God continues to speak—to Noah, to Abraham, to Moses, to Joshua, to Elisha, and to many others. This continues moving forward to King David, his son Solomon, the prophets, and finally to Jesus, and through Jesus, who was fully human, God continues to speak to us, for after Jesus the conversation continued through Paul and the other apostles, and then through the New Testament to all of us today.

Many people think of the Old Testament as less than the New Testament. They read the violence on its pages and the way God speaks, and they miss the love, which sometimes is "tough love."

God really begins his most focused work with us through Abraham. Abraham would not pass muster as a good human in our modern world. He tried to save his own skin by passing off his wife as his sister on more than one occasion. He needed constant encouragement to keep doing as God commanded him. We might even call him shiftless—especially in the early years of his conversations with God.

In my own experience with God, I can empathize with Abram, his name before God's last covenant with him. I was raised as a nominal Christian in a nominal Christian family. I got other values at some level and especially when I became a singer in the Dallas-Fort Worth area. Women began to come through my life. As I have written earlier, I didn't know how to have a relationship with them, and this left me feeling guilty. I knew that I should feel something and that I should treat women with honor, and I just didn't know how.

I began to talk to God in a new way as part of my conversation with him. Earlier, I would say "God if you are there," and then tell him why I needed him to be there. At this time—which was before I went on the road as a singer—I just told him I didn't like the life that I was living, and I said to Him that I didn't know how to stop that lifestyle. I said to Him, "If you want me to change, you will have to change me yourself, or at least show me how to change."

Nothing happened—at least not then—but the events around my dad's heart attack and surgery, when I began to fly back from Houston every week and when he spoke to my family in the chapel at Harris Hospital in Fort Worth, were beginning to get my attention. I was just as shiftless as Abram seemed to be in the beginning of his conversation with God. So I think I understand Abram. I understand how hard it is to change just because God is calling to you. I had my ways and those ways define me as a person. How do you get redefined—to yourself? to others? to God? As I have written earlier, it all came to a head at another gig, in another hotel, in another city, and then my conversation with God continued.

God kept talking to the Hebrew people. All of the patriarchs were less than what we demand of people today. They were also a savage people—given to violence toward others. Much of the violence of the Old Testament is just the ancient Hebrews being themselves.

These violent people were the clay from which God had fashioned his people to prepare them for the time of the Messiah.

First God talked to them through those who carried on the "oral traditions" and then to those who wrote on scrolls like those found in jars by the Dead Sea. Someone heard the words, and then someone else retold or wrote down the words of God to his people.

Many times the words were a scathing rebuke, for his people kept turning from Him to foreign gods or even to no gods at all. In the midst of all these words to his people were ones like these:

Hear, O Israel: The Lord is our God, the Lord alone. You shall love the Lord your God with all your heart, and with all your soul, and with all your might. Keep these words that I am commanding you today in your heart... (Deuteronomy 6:4–6)

I demand mercy and not sacrifice. (Hosea 6:6)

He has told you, O mortal, what is good; and what does the Lord require of you but to do justice, and to love kindness, and to walk humbly with your God? (Micah 6:8)

When Israel was a child, I loved him, and out of Egypt I called my son. The more I called them, the more they went from me. They kept sacrificing to the Baals, and offering incense to idols. Yet it was I who taught Ephraim to walk. I took them in my arms; But they did not know that I healed them. I led them with cords of human kindness, with bands of love. I was to them like those who lift infants to their cheeks. I bent down to them and fed them—Because they have refused to return to me the sword rages in their cities... How can I give you up, Ephraim? How can I hand you over, O Israel? How can I make you like Admah? How can I treat you like Zeboliim? My heart recoils within me. I will not execute my fierce anger; I will not again destroy Ephraim; for I am God and no mortal, the Holy One in your midst. (Hosea 11:1–9)

God didn't mince words when he was angry, but neither did he mince words when he was showing how filled he was with love for his people.

The New Testament God is not a new God. God is God in the Old Testament, in the New Testament, and now. He is just always moving by the Holy Spirit to teach us what it means to be children of God and members of the household of God. We can still be savage people in these times after the New Testament—witness the bloody wars waged in his name from the Crusades until the Inquisition, the conquering of the New World, and more recently in the United Kingdom and in Ireland.

Moreover, we still don't understand that the conversation God wants with us is about one of the first choices in all of human history—the choice between good and evil.

Modern Christianity is obsessed with being good—which we can't be. (Paul: "I do not do the good I want, but the evil I do not want is what I do" [Romans 7:19].) And growing in faith requires that we now love at a level that most push aside as impossible. We fail to deal with our basic evil nature, and although we preach grace, we misunderstand the call of grace to do that very deep love of God that we can't imagine doing.

In the Beatitudes and the Sermon on the Mount of Matthew (chapters 5 to 7), Jesus calls us out for our very thoughts and casual behavior in condemning others with cruel epithets. In other places in the New Testament, our cruel tongues are what amount to weapons of destruction.

The selfishness and self-centeredness that lives in us is the evil Jesus speaks of when he says of the disciples, "you who are evil" (Matthew 7:11–12). It is also the "darkness" in which we walk around according to the Apostle John in John 3:19: "And this is the judgment, that the light has come into the world, and people lived darkness rather than light because their deeds were evil."

This darkness permeates the ground and air around us, and we spread it like a virus. Without a rudder to guide us as we navigate this world, where success is so often measured by our wealth in money and things, we are put into competition with those around us. So Jesus in the Sermon on the Mount cautions us not to even call our brother a fool, or we will be in danger of hellfire. Likewise, he says that holding thoughts of adultery in our hearts is to have already committed that act in our hearts.

How can we not do these things? We can't escape them, but Jesus gives the answer when he says that "for men it is impossible, but all things are possible with God" (Matthew 19:26).

When God says to Moses that he should take off his shoes for he is walking on holy ground, it is because God is there, and his goodness is all around and in everything. But it is also true that our evilness is all around and in everything. The kingdom is far out of our reach because of this, and we can't focus on the "treasure in a field" or the "pearl of great price" (Matthew 13:44–46).

Yet if we daily—even minute by minute—surrender to Christ and, if we die to self, then with him in us, we become a carrier of goodness and not evil. The world around us will be a sea of evil while we will be an island of God's peace.

Marriages in the western world fall apart, and then are often followed by more failure after remarriages so that some say that we practice serial polygamy.

Perhaps if we understood the evil we do to each other in the name of love, and if we would try harder to grasp how much goodness could exist in us because of the grace of God, we would converse with him more honestly, and our relationships would grow rather than fail.

The key here is honest conversation with God about the possibility of good and evil in us. Our selfish and self-centered natures cause us to be takers more than givers, and we want others to please us and want life in general to be good to us.

THE BIBLE AS A LOVE LETTER
FROM GOD TO HIS CHILDREN

The Bible is viewed in many ways. However, I believe that God only meant his holy book to be viewed as a communication of his enduring love for his children.

To use the Bible as a legal brief with which to beat folks over the head with "Thou shalt not" or "Obey this commandment, or you are going to go to hell" is absolutely wrong. And to use the Bible to mine scriptures with which to build various theologies for women, Blacks, gays, etc., does violence to God's intent with his book. God knows of all injustice to all people, and the Bible's call for loving others as ourselves (great commandment) is sufficient to cover all groups, wanting to pull out scriptures to justify special attention to injustice done to them.

The Bible is a history of the mighty acts of God in bringing his wayward children back to him and a call for us to pattern our lives after his love for us. Jesus's call for us to "be perfect therefore, as your Heavenly Father is perfect"(Matthew 5:48) is just what he expects of us. And as long as we can focus on this call to perfection as a journey taken one step at a time, and not a destination that we must attain today, or really ever in this lifetime, then it should not be an undue burden.

John and Charles Wesley talked of the attainability of perfection in love, by which they meant that we can be so focused on the journey to perfection that even when we fall off of the path, we are quickly led back on by the Holy Spirit, who is always there with us.

"For what the flesh wants is opposed to the Spirit, and what the Spirit wants is opposed to the flesh. They are opposed to each other, and so you do not do what you want to do" (Galatians 5:17).

The Old Testament is a history from creation until New Testament times of God patiently preparing the way for the Messiah. God's word in the book of Hosea is a good example as he lays his charge against Israel for their wantonness with other gods and the wayward and earthly lifestyle of the people. Then in chapter 6:6, he tells them that to be true to him is not about their empty sacrifices offered up in his name (he hates those because of their emptiness) but about mercy. By "mercy," God means that his children should act toward others with the same mercy/loving kindness/righteousness that he has shown to them.

Then in chapter 11:1–9, he shows his love for them by baring his heart to them:

> When Israel was a child I loved him and out of Egypt I called my son. But the more I called Israel the further they went from me. They sacrificed to the Baals and they burned incense to images.
>
> It was I who taught Ephraim to walk, taking them by the arms, but they did not realize it was I who healed them. I led them with cords of human kindness with ties of love. I lifted the yoke from their neck and bent down to feed them. Will they not return to Egypt? and will not Assyria rule over them, because they refuse to repent… My people are determined to turn from me. Even if they call to the Most High he will by no means exalt them.
>
> How can I give you up, Ephraim? How can I hand you over, Israel? How can I treat you like Admah? How can I make you like Zeboiim? My heart is changed within me. All my compassion is aroused. I will not carry out my fierce anger nor will I turn and devastate Ephraim, for I am God and not man, the Holy One among you.

Jesus quotes Hosea in Matt hew9:13 when asked why he dines with Matthew the tax collector and with other sinners. And then he hears his disciples being asked why he does so.

His reply is, "It is not the healthy that need a doctor, but the sick. But go and learn what this means, 'I desire mercy, and not sacrifice.' For I have not come to call the righteous, but sinners" (Luke 5:32).

So here and in the Old Testament, God is saying, "My people show they are mine by how they treat each other."

We read this in John 13:34: "A new Command I give you: As I have loved you, so you must love one another. By this all men will know that you are my disciples, if you have love for one another."

Listen to John 3:16 (for God so gave his only begotten son…) or the great commandment (Mark 12:28–31—I choose this version over Matthew's because this is a quote from Deuteronomy 6:4 and Leviticus 19:18).

So here you find a quick overview of God's demands on us, and we can sum it up with Matthew 5:48: "Be perfect, therefore, as your heavenly Father is perfect."

THE BIBLE AS A CHALLENGE FROM GOD TO HIS CHILDREN

Jesus went through one town and village after another, teaching as he made his way to Jerusalem. Someone asked him, "Lord, will only a few be saved?" He said to them, "Strive to enter through the narrow door; for many, I tell you, will try to enter and will not be able. When once the owner of the house has got up and shut the door, and you begin to stand outside and to knock at the door, saying, 'Lord, open to us,' then in reply he will say to you, 'I do not know where you come from.' Then you will begin to say, 'We ate and drank with you, and you taught in our streets.' [27] But he will say, 'I do not know where you come from; go away from me, all you evildoers!' [28] There will be weeping and gnashing of teeth when you see Abraham and Isaac and Jacob and all the prophets in the kingdom of God, and you yourselves thrown out. [29] Then people will come from east and west, from north and south, and will eat in the kingdom of God. [30] Indeed, some are last who will be first, and some are first who will be last. (Luke 13:30)

Do not suppose that I have come to bring peace to the earth. *I did not come to bring peace, but a sword.* For I have come to turn "a man against his father, a daughter against her mother, a daughter-in-law against her mother-in-law—a man's enemies will be the members of his own household." (Matthew 10:34– 36, emphasis mine)

Someone told him, "Your mother and brothers are standing outside, wanting to speak to you." He replied to him, "Who is *my mother*, and who are *my brothers*?" Pointing to his disciples, he said, "Here are my mother *and* my brothers. For whoever does the will of my Father in heaven is *my* brother and sister and mother." (Matthew 12:47–50, emphasis mine)

The angels cried out that Jesus came to bring peace on earth and goodwill among men. Jesus says that he came to bring a sword. What can this mean? I believe it has to do with how we receive his words and then what we do with them.

Those who take his words to heart and try to live by them will find themselves held at distance by others unless they become very dedicated to serving others (walk the walk). Enough dedication to service will get a person a good kind of notoriety, but they will have a hard time explaining why they do what they do. Why? Because people do not want to hear the truth of the kingdom; it requires more giving of ourselves than most people want to be open to.

Who among us wants to love our enemies, or forgive like God does, or be last in order to be first? Who wants to give up all that we have, or at the very least be fully prepared to do so, in order to find the peace of Christ?

Jesus came to offer us what we see as an uncomfortable way of living that nevertheless offers us divine comfort. He calls us to dare to be different in a way that the sword will separate us from some of those closest to us.

When John and Charles Wesley began to teach perfection in love, they were vehemently disagreed with for believing, much less teaching, such doctrine.

Jesus made a very uncomfortable response to someone saying that his mother and brothers were wishing to see him. The comforting thing to say would have been "bring them to me." Instead, he changed the subject; people must have thought, *How dare he belittle the institution of family.*

But he did this to say what was of more importance than anything else in life. It was just like the parables of the pearl of great price or the treasure in a field. He was holding up the kingdom as the most ultimate of all things to be looked for, and it brought division, it brought a sword, even between his family and himself. One who moves toward giving all of the self will eventually be seen for the godly person they are, but the journey will include the heartache of being misunderstood along the way.

Evil is real, and it is an entity that stands between us, the people created by God for God, and between us and God himself. It, or Satan, is in a losing but protracted and often violent war with the goodness of God.

Does this evil that Jesus called the "Prince of this world" (John 14:30) have other fallen angels or demons following him, and how do they manifest it in this modern world? It is hard to see just how demons might function in the world today, but Satan, at least, is clearly the manifestation of evil even now. At the least, Satan is against love winning out and will do all that he can in order to prevent the inevitable doom of his own cause.

Modern medicine and psychology can explain much of why we fail at love, but we know within ourselves that our decisions and actions often defy our own understanding. Modern psychological and neurological information about us can't explain all of what we do or why we do it. When we push past anger at someone into rage against them and when we like those raging feelings, where did that come from? Can psychology or neurology fully explain all of that?

Our souls are kingdom-created and kingdom-oriented, but at the same time, they are vulnerable to evil. At the soul level, unconditional love is offered as the path to our best, and evil works to defeat that kingdom-best with self-oriented feelings that at the very least fall short of God's glory. At the worst, Satan wants us in full rebellion against God. So at this level, we are all about good and evil, and which will win out? Will it be the godliness of our kingdom family, or will it be the absolute opposite, which is the despair of eternal damnation? Will it more likely be a path of confused feelings about what God expects of us, where we excuse ourselves as merely human? Then, as merely human God shouldn't hold our lack of soul-deep honesty with him against us.

After all, we have a life to live with other people who wouldn't understand if we put the kingdom before them, like Jesus did with his family.

Or are there other considerations? Is there a purgatory, a place to be given another chance if we fail here? Could it even be that God will eventually win all to himself through a purgatory-like place?

Christians disagree vehemently about these things, but we mostly agree that evil wants to separate us from God. So at a soul level, there is a whole different conversation going on than in the broad world of daily living. This conversation is all too often about whether or not we will ever be good enough to go to heaven "in the sweet bye-and-bye," and not nearly enough about growing spiritually closer to God in the present time. It is rarely ever about exchanging eternity for time as our reference point instead of the here and now.

I find it hard to picture living in the kingdom now until I engage in the acts of love and giving that I have talked about. These things warm my heart and cause me to feel God's presence all around me. The kingdom comes to me, not so much as a place but as an experience. It is a warmer way of being with and around others. It gives purpose to my being, and I say to God, "Without you, I have no purpose, but with you, I know why I live and breathe."

Jesus called the Jews of his day an evil generation because they had succumbed to a culture guided by thousands of laws. These were directions for living based on the law of Moses and enforced and added to by the Pharisees and Sadducees.

We have all probably heard the modern parable that says we all have two dogs within us; one is good and the other is evil, and the question is which one will guide our lives. The answer is, of course, "It will be the one we feed."

Living by the law of Moses and all the little add-on laws of their culture kept the Jews at the mercy of temptation. Paul said it this way:

> I do not understand my own actions. For I do not do what
> I want, but I do the very thing I hate. For I know that nothing
> good dwells within me, that is, in my flesh. I can will what

is right, but I cannot do it... Now if I do what I do not want,
it is no longer I that do it, but sin that lives within me.
(Romans 7:15–20)

That sounds a lot like "the devil made me do it" and, in a way of
speaking, it is true. Our souls are eternal, of the kingdom and in the
kingdom, and yet are swayed against God's holy way by the force of
evil that rages against the kingdom being realized "on earth as it is
in heaven."

We aren't usually aware of the kingdom nature of our souls, but
we should be. We call the part of us that decides to be good or bad
(we don't want to associate ourselves with the possibility of being
evil) our conscience. This keeps our understanding of our behavior
on a worldly plane, and we don't have to consider God in the
equation. That is good for our peace of mind because when we dig
down to the soul level, as Jesus does when he says that even "calling
a brother a fool" puts us in danger of hellfire, we might be horrified
at how much we hurt ourselves and others at a spiritual level.

So what I believe that Jesus means is that calling a brother a fool
is a soul problem and not one of the conscience or of worldly
practice. It is a question of which dog to feed. Will it be the worldly,
and will we dismiss the evil that tempts us? Or will we see our
behavioral decisions and actions as of great consequence to our walk
with God and the building of the kingdom of God on earth—what
we say and do after all?

There is a worldly way of getting an approximation of what our
souls may be doing with the information that we glean just from
living and moving about in this world, and even in a way that our
spirits glean from relating to God, others, and evil. It is called the
Johari window (proposed by psychologists Joseph Luft and
Harrington Ingham and named by using parts of their first names).

Imagine a four-paned window where the upper-left pane holds
those things we know of ourselves and that others know of us also.
The upper-right pane holds things that we don't know of ourselves
but others do. The lower-left pane holds things we know of ourselves

but others don't. And the lower-right pane then holds things that neither we nor others know of ourselves.

It is the lower-right pane that has gotten much attention from researchers of human consciousness. Could this be our subconscious minds? Is this the place that dreams come from? Is this where those random thoughts come from that catch us off guard and we say, "Where did that come from"?

Or is this the storehouse of those things known to our souls and mostly hidden from our conscious selves until they can be useful? Some say, for example, that dreams are a way of processing stuff from the subconscious mind.

What if this is a soul storehouse? It would then be the battleground where good and evil thoughts fight it out. It would be the place that the Apostle Paul is calling the "sin that lives within me." Sure, our conscious minds have to respond to and process what comes up from the subconscious, but where did the push for good and evil start? Did this push come from the forces of good and evil in our souls, and then come up into our unconscious minds? Is the unconscious/subconscious mind our very souls?

Neuroscientists will no doubt point to the brain map and say that all emotions come from the limbic system where chemicals and hormones affect our behavior. If we are only animals with our behaviors determined by the combined stimuli of life, I would accept this. But if we are, as Christians and others believe, children of God and made in his image, then a glandular/chemical/hormonal explanation of spiritual happenings falls very short of eternal truth.

So if there are eternal truths about good and evil, then there must be eternal behaviors that help us be children of light as John speaks of in John 12:36: "Believe in the light while you have the light, so that you may become children of light." We have Jesus with us all the time by the help of the Holy Spirit, and we are offered a way of cleansing our souls from evil and fighting off attacks from evil.

Walking the path of love long enough and sincerely enough is the way to grow into being children of the light, or to put this thought in the words of John Wesley: "Do all the good you can, by all the means you can, in all the ways you can, in all the places you can, at all the times you can, to all the people you can, as long as ever you can."

There is a hole in each of our hearts. Love for another is a matter of them filling needs for warmth, trust, emotional, and even spiritual needs that we have so that we cannot imagine living without them. Let's say that we have an oval-shaped hole in us and the one we love has a square shape so that they never entirely fit the hole at the center of our emotional selves. There is a good reason for that, for the hole is shaped such that only God can totally fill it. It then stands to reason that the more godly we become, the better we will fit into each other's beingness. So growing apart happens when we stop being vulnerable to God and others.

We are created in the image of God; we are made to be like him. Therefore, we are called by him to be like him (be perfect as your Father is perfect [Matthew 5:48]). If we are not actively seeking God's kingdom, we cannot possibly grasp the call to perfection and the grace of God that makes it possible for us to walk that path.

CHAPTER 4

Living in the Now with Kingdom Eyes

The purpose of exploring the spiritual life is that it should be our primary quest in life. Jesus has taught us to love as he loves us and to seek first the kingdom of God as opposed to seeking things or fame and fortune. What we need and even much of what we want (providing it is healthy for us spiritually) will then be given us. The problem is one of focus. Keeping our focus on the kingdom is what I call kingdom eyes, and we are constantly being distracted by the world.

Examples of Kingdom Eyes

Let us begin with more on "kingdom eyes," what I mean by that term, and some examples of how this works in our lives in this world.

God created all things and is still creating, and we, as members of the heavenly family, are invited to be creating also. It is true that you and I will almost surely never move a bush or a mountain while alive in this world, but that is so only because of our perception of reality. We live too much in this world and not enough in the eternal kingdom. This eternal kingdom is here all around us and, if we had kingdom eyes, we would see it and operate within it as well as within this world.

Flashes of the kingdom do appear to us throughout our lives if we are open to it. When someone such a little girl in Keller, Texas, befriends a special needs child with cerebral palsy as her best friend, you already have a special young lady. When this same girl sends a letter to the city council asking that they modify a playground that the two attend so that her friend can enjoy it also, God is certainly in the picture. Then when the city council doesn't answer her plea, the girl goes on to stand before the council and make her plea in person. She got her wish—the council added a swing designed to be used by a child with cerebral palsy. If I were standing by that girl as she stood up out of love for her friend, then I would know that I was standing on holy ground.

Suzie and I are recently back from Scotland, and while there we went to the island of Iona and worshipped in the ancient abbey on the isle. It was truly a holy moment also. Then we crossed Scotland from west to east, went through Edinburgh, and then south to the island of Lindisfarne in the north of England. Here it was that the Irish monk, Aidan, brought Christianity to the kingdom of Northumbria. This island is better known as Holy Island throughout England and Scotland. In fact, my WeatherBug phone app brought it up as Holy Island. Each of these islands is also known as a "thin place." They are places where God and the kingdom just feel closer than at other places.

THE EXAMPLE OF AIDAN

Aidan came to the kingdom of Northumbria at the request of its king to bring Christianity as the king had witnessed it on the island of Iona when he was in exile there. What Aidan brought was a loving and personal faith of the type that St. Francis brought to Assisi. He requested the tidal island of Lindisfarne as his headquarters, and so began such a loving ministry that the reverberations of that love echo still today. Aidan walked out among the people of the kingdom and became as one with them. He was with them in love as an emissary of God, and they felt God's love through him, and they believed.

With the Holy Spirit in him, Aidan exceeded himself, and Lindisfarne became holy ground then and now. You can feel God's closeness as you approach the island, and Suzie and I, along with the others in our group of travelers, got to sit and listen to some of the community of Aidan and Hilda (Hilda is another Celtic saint) as they unpacked their gentle and loving faith for us. Their sharing was gentle yet powerful, and that same quiet yet persistent power was all around us on the island. God was with us, and we knew it. God didn't show himself through overt miracles, but we were offered eyes to see God's kingdom, ears to hear his still small voice, and our hearts were filled with wonder at all the ways he spoke to us there.

Response to Holy Island and Lifestyle Today

Suzie and I have begun to talk about our experience on Holy Island and what we should take away from it. Can we see the gain in letting God be in charge of our future instead of dreaming of a Caribbean lifestyle? Are we prepared to hand God all of who we are and all of our stuff, and then take whatever he gives back? Will that work for us? We intend to plunge ahead and find out, and we will start by being more of a team instead of mostly following my lead.

Now let me admit, I often say that it is my hand that is on the rudder of our family ship. Some take that to mean that I dominate Suzie. Nothing could be further from the truth, as over our sixteen years together, whatever chauvinism that was in me has given way to my desire to help Suzie become all that she can be. Our house and the property that it sits on demonstrates that. Our wooded backyard and the deck that was on the back of the house when we bought it have gone through many changes. Most of those changes made on our house and property have been made because I perceived that Suzie wanted them or needed them. Mostly I have been right, although my version of what she wanted hasn't always looked to her like what she had in mind.

I am more grandiose than Suzie. She wanted a screen porch on the back of our house. I worked with her brother-in-law's drawings and a team of carpenters to build a twelve-by-twenty-four-foot room that follows the contours of the house and is now fully enclosed. It is now our dining room and bedroom. As a screen porch, it was much bigger than Suzie wanted, and then we found out we couldn't use it yearround, and thus it was reinvented. Now, as a bedroom and dining room, it is highly usable, and we both love it. It took over a year, but our visions came together, and we both got what we wanted.

Am I in charge of our lives, as many of our friends believe, or is God working in both of us to show us how to be a team?

When we first met, Suzie looked at me as, in her words, bigger than life. I saw her as someone who needed to become all that she could be, and I told her that I, who had always been an outsider, could see much of myself in her as she had always been an outsider as well. I had faced many of my character flaws because of God's work in me. I had asked God to help me drop my defenses that isolated me so much, and then I asked for the Holy Spirit to become my defense.

Suzie and I met, and I could see how letting go and letting that same spirit teach me how to love her would also free her to risk trusting herself to love me. So she said, "Let me love you as I can," to which I, with the help of God, opened myself to trust that she could overcome her trust issues and really love me.

The next morning, I woke with a vision of her and me walking out to eternity together. And then when I foolishly questioned God about whether she could actually learn to love herself and then me, another thing happened. I told Suzie that we had a journey to attend together, and she said, "Yes, we have a path to be on." Journey or path, it was all the same, and we began that walk together.

I have mentioned my lack of urgency throughout my life. Some would call that a laidback attitude, and I can accept that description, but I find it interesting that some of our friends suggest that I have on blinders and that I am always in my head and miss out on what is happening around me. There is a lot of truth in that, and if so, it is all part of my lack of urgency—my laidback/into-self ways.

I would say that all of this is a part of my defenses, but there is a difference in that when I am into myself, I am very often praying to God for the openness to others that I lack. Then, when you look at the love Martin UMC showed me at my recent retirement, you can see that I was able to open myself to them to the extent that they felt loved by me even as I still struggle with that openness.

When I was entertaining, I always did best when people opened up to me first. If I hit on the right songs and did them well enough that they would cheer me on, I would exceed myself in being open to them.

I find that some of the same things happened in my ministry at Martin. Martin is a loving church, and they accepted me immediately. My hospital visits helped because somehow God just shows through me more there than elsewhere, and maybe that is because it is a dedicated ministry. You both know that you are there to share God's love, compassion, and prayers for his healing touch. I always feel close to those I visit in hospitals, nursing homes, or retirement centers.

Another place God in me is apparent to others is when I teach or when I pray in public. Teaching is a freeing experience for me as I get excited and animated in the process. Then, when I share the very things I am writing about here, it is clear that I am caught up in sharing God's love for us and God's call on us.

The discussion about my holding the rudder of my marriage has been revisited since going to Scotland and then to Holy Island. It is time now to let the Holy Spirit open both Suzie and me to a deeper walk than we have been willing to risk up until this time. It is also time to be more intentional about what our shared roles are and how we can let God use us going forward.

"REALITY"

Reality for each of us is what we perceive it to be. As we grow in Christ Jesus and in his love, our perception of reality changes. We see the world with growing kingdom eyes, and the world and our place in it changes. Our ears open up more, and we hear God's voice in ways we couldn't before—in the music of the ocean breeze, the song of a bird, and the cry of a baby. Our hearts are softened, we can forgive and forget offenses against us, and we become more like Jesus—we are on the narrow road.

The call to love as Jesus loved us, or as our God himself loves us, seems at least to be something we can move toward. We are moving into the kingdom on earth as it is in heaven, and we may even know it.

So what is reality? If we take it to mean the physical world around us, the question is, how do we relate to it? If we are moving into the "kingdom on earth as it is in heaven," then our relationship to the physical world may be changing. As we view and experience our surroundings through kingdom eyes, ears, and heart, everything takes on a different meaning, and again our perception of reality itself changes.

Hopeless situations do not have to be hopeless anymore. It becomes possible to revisit broken relationships with the Holy Spirit to help us to exceed ourselves in love. The world and all of its problems may not have changed, but we who are changed can now see how, one relationship at a time and one loving act at a time, we can let God in us make a difference. Like Aidan, by our love shared with others, it is possible that other places—even the space around us—can become "thin places."

FORGIVENESS

When the subject of forgiveness comes up, you will almost always hear someone say, "I can forgive, but I can't forget." Similarly, people will say that they can't turn the other cheek, walk the extra mile, give their shirt as well as their cloak, etc.

As the seventy disciples said upon hearing Jesus speak in John's gospel of eating his flesh and drinking his blood, we may say something like "These are hard sayings." It is hard for us to imagine what Jesus can mean by these sayings and also by "Be perfect as your heavenly Father is perfect." Yet it is in this direction that we need to be asking the Holy Spirit to guide us.

Granted, we must hear the Spirit's prompting to even ask for such guidance to begin with. If this sounds like circular reasoning, consider that the Holy Spirit is constantly reaching out to us to hear God's call for us to be like him. When we leave a crack open for the Spirit to get in, then he will seek to widen that crack. Then when we ask for help, the crack is opened even wider, and if we make it our main purpose in life to serve God with all of our "heart and with all our soul and with all of our minds," then the narrow kingdom gate is thrust open still wider for us to serve God's kingdom in this world.

Here is where many of us stumble and struggle. We may have questions like: Where do I begin? Where do I go to find someone with whom to walk an extra mile? Do I jump right in the middle of this part of the conversation on good and evil by selling all my worldly possessions, like St Francis did, and then giving it all to the needy? Do I abandon my family as the disciples did?

The answer to those hard questions may be found in the nature of God's call on our individual lives. St Francis and many other saints heard that extreme call and answered it. Still, St. Francis told a whole village that wanted to follow him that they couldn't abandon their lives en masse and follow him. Instead, he gave them a systematic set of rules to use for guidance in daily living.

I believe that living a holier life for you and me is to just surrender to the process of asking for instruction from the Spirit as we feel him in our lives prompting us to do so. He will guide us to the next step that we have the capacity to take. If we don't fear that step, then we probably haven't heard what he is saying. This is like giving a tithe. If the amount we give doesn't hurt to some degree, then it is most likely not enough to bring about change in our lives.

My history suggests that God will lead me if I will listen to the Spirit and then attempt to follow. At the very least, that means to follow the central commandment of the gospel—the great commandment and Jesus's commandment to love as found in the Gospel of John. If we attempt to follow it, the commandment to love softens our hearts toward others—even to people we don't like. As our hearts are softened, then little by little, we can feel the possibility that we can be more like God. We can accept that God's grace can change us in ways that demonstrate to us and to others that we are being remade in the image of God himself.

Looking Back to Look Forward

Now I will change from reflection to forward-looking as Suzie and I ask God for direction going forward. Yet it is also time to share some of my early visions, if only for motivation for me to risk more for Christ and to help you who read this to walk with us.

So, in the fall of 1975, I was often in a darkened hotel room. Darkened, because when I wasn't working in the bar as an entertainer, I was usually in that room meditating and whining to God about how I just didn't fit in this world. I would tell God that my lifestyle was against his ways and that I couldn't change it myself. I had a girlfriend in Arlington, Texas, to whom I was never true. She had a friend whom I had blatantly flirted with in front of her, and I was always looking around for some other female distraction. So you understand how messed up my prayers were and just how self-serving they were. Yes, my life was all about me, but if God would just fix me, then he and I could be closer.

So I was saying that I don't belong in this world, and suddenly, in my meditation, I am traveling through space on a destination to see God and then die in this world. I passed a point clearly marked as the point of no return, and I found myself apologizing to God profusely for my selfishness. I wasn't afraid because I felt his love and compassion for me, even though it was clear that I in no way deserved it. I was getting close to some place which I saw as a planet, and that doesn't mean that God is on a planet. But it was just the best my mind could imagine about what he was showing me. Then the phone rang.

My girlfriend in Arlington had gotten a phone call from her friend whom I had flirted with, and the friend had said, "Jim is in trouble, and you need to call him." Well, my girlfriend didn't believe her, so the friend had gotten got my number and called me in a panic. I picked up the phone and the first words that I heard were "Whatever you are doing, stop it."

I knew then that God's love for me was deep enough that he wouldn't just stop me in limbo and reject me, but he would and could call me back from this world—and He did. He was giving me a renewed chance to let him help me see myself as the selfish and completely self-centered person that I was. And then he would help me grow out of myself for his sake.

Unfortunately, I had to involve myself with one more woman, saying to myself that surely she was the one, although I knew that I was just using her like a drug, and when she saw that too, it was over.

So after I got off the bandstand the next night, I went to my room and fell into bed and into a deep sleep immediately. Immediately, I was in the dark side of a moonlike landscape, and I felt that God had thrown me away. I cried out to him in fear—yes, into much fear and trembling. I felt that I had finally gone too far against the will of God and that he was through with me. No doubt, like dreams, the actual time of this happening was only a few minutes, but it seemed like forever. Then I suddenly felt released from judgment and set free to try to follow him again.

That is a large part of what drives me forward in Christ, for in both visions I was loved by God in spite of my selfish self. My life had been all about pleasing and soothing myself. I needed to hide from my feeling of "less than." I did it with alcohol and the search for the "perfect woman." I would, of course, not have known her even if I had found her, and if by chance the perfect lady had come to me, I would have soon moved on because I was not ready to see others, men or women, as God's children. I couldn't even see myself as a child of God. So I didn't treat anyone, even myself, with respect and certainly not with love.

Out of my plea for God to reveal my darkest self to me, even if I died, came the acknowledgment of money borrowed and not paid back as something to pray for forgiveness. All whom I borrowed from are now dead.

The bow waves of self-protection coming off me like a ship on the sea held back God's spirit from showing through me. Some said that I had blinders to all I didn't want to see so that I didn't notice much of what was going on around me. I was too often lost in my own thoughts. What did I miss and how many missed the chance of feeling the Spirit through me? A huge amount of the angst and even evil in this world is caused by withholding ourselves from God and then from others.

It is true that we need some protection from others and from the world in the early stages of spiritual growth. I once said that God is the only being in the universe who can stand in the wind of all human emotion and survive that onslaught. Too much exposure to others' emotions could and would overwhelm us early in our spiritual development, and even Jesus needed time to recharge his emotional/spiritual self after giving through teaching and healing and through the spiritual weight of people's need for him to fix them.

I have heard it said in sermons and in seminary lessons that encountering Jesus would cause people to examine themselves to the bottom of their souls because of his goodness showing up their evil in ways they could not deny. God is all-powerful and yet vulnerable. He created us to have us mirror that vulnerability for the world to see him, and yet all of us—including myself—withhold ourselves from others on too many occasions. God opened himself to us in Jesus, so let us open ourselves to others.

It is dangerous to try to extrapolate God's nature from human traits, but we can look for the perfect in how we exercise the imperfect. For example, we use power to protect ourselves. We also use this power to hold on to what is ours. Psychopaths and sociopaths don't need an excuse to exercise power since they feel power over others is theirs by right.

God is power and is so secure in his power that he can give it away. This is unlike John Calvin's understanding of God as so almighty that he couldn't give any of it away—thus, no free will for humankind.

Men are confused by the emotions of women, especially when what sets off those emotions may feel so trivial to men. Women are surprised by men being confused, irritated, or even angry just because they expect men to know what they feel and what they need—expecting men to read their minds—or to get in touch with the woman's emotions without them being expressed verbally. Feelings of being safely home are different for men and women.

Withholding ourselves, not noticing others, and not listening to others in a way that they are aware of being listened to is counterproductive— as when Suzie is sharing with me and I appear engrossed in something else even as I hear every word. That is not a quality moment for her. Group conversation where no one is willing to be exposed in an honest way falls short of being a quality sharing. These are certainly the safe ways of being in conversation, but they fail to hold back evil in the way that true sharing does. Such distracted (or at least not-engaged) conversation gives tacit agreement to letting evil stay buried and not addressed.

Within months after my call to ministry was cemented by my fearful acceptance, I felt God calling for a deeper acceptance of himself, and I quickly turned that into God's calling for me to be different. I had always been a loner, awkward in social settings, and now I felt that I would have to be even more different. I couldn't do that. I pulled back from God, not quitting the call but putting on a layer of protection from him. I know I didn't get an image of a vindictive and heavy-fisted God from my Methodist upbringing. But neither did I get an understanding of God's grace. I couldn't see that if he gives you a high calling, he will also give you the ability to fulfill that calling. It was only much later that I further realized that the call is absolute. We are truly called to be perfect as he is perfect. That is the absolute, but his grace helps us to put our feet on that journey, and he leads us a step at a time. We are not even called to be perfect in this world, for the journey leads on into the next stage of the kingdom experience.

Still, John and Charles Wesley taught that some could reach perfection in love. These were those who had so deeply accepted God's call on their lives that they would stick to the narrow path and, when they fell off in a self-centered moment, they would quickly allow God to help them back on the right path.

It takes a moment of spiritual serendipity to get us, his children, on such a path, but I think of the woman told about in the Gospel of John who was caught in adultery. She clearly knew she deserved to be stoned, as per God's wrath for her sin. Yet Jesus, who came to die for sins such as hers, showed the very grace he came to embody by doing for her what she could not do for herself. He forgave her when she could not, under the law, have ever forgiven herself, and in that moment, he gave her the opportunity to get on the path to the kingdom knowing he would be there to help her when she fell off. Was she able to appropriate that grace into her life? The Bible does not tell us the rest of her story, but I like to think that she did, in fact, begin her journey from there.

Wesley's call for Christian perfection caused me pause— especially after I answered that very same call at my ordination. The bishop asked me if I intended to go on to perfection, and I am sure I wasn't alone in wondering what that would mean in my life.

My sins are still of the kind that hunt others without my intent. I am not yet open emotionally on all occasions, and I still sometimes miss hearing the real needs of others when they really need me to hear them. I work at being present—really hearing others in a way that they feel heard down into their souls. That was Jesus's way, and I must admit that I am just on the journey to such a way of hearing and being present. I am up-front with God about my lacking in this area of truly hearing others. In fact, this subject goes back to the beginning of this book: *love is everything, and being present for others is love in action.*

REFLECTIONS ON MINISTRY AT MARTIN UMC

Now let us move into the more recent past and the present. Much of what I have been teaching at Martin United Methodist Church has been preparation for this book. I chose to teach from a book by M. Scott Peck, *The Road Less Traveled*; C. S. Lewis's books *Mere Christianity* and *The Great Divorce*, Richard Rohr's video series on spiritual growth and one he calls *The Change That Changes Everything*. We also studied the Gospel of John using William Barclay's book as our guide. I also wrote several eight-week series that combined ideas from both of Rohr's video series. It was during another eight-week series on Celtic Christianity taught by my friend and old college professor, Jesse Sowell, that I became aware of the debt we owe to these folks for lighting the way for a closer walk with Christ for those who take the time to study them.

All of these authors helped those who studied with me to be open to new thoughts and faith paths in each of our journeys. Scott Peck began his book by saying that, "Life is difficult." He goes on to say that unless we face into that difficulty, we will not find our way to satisfaction in life.

He lays out a really good case for facing ourselves and others with integrity and honesty. It would seem that such a path would be easy to intuit, but he says that too many of us want life to be fair and/or we give in to various neurosis that separate us from our own possible selves as well as from others. I give this very incomplete synopsis only to show how my class began our walk together. We looked at ourselves and how we chose to relate to others.

The C. S. Lewis books let us into his own walk from atheist to Christian, and all of us could see in his questions some that we had asked of ourselves and of God. Each book we studied then caused us to look into ourselves in ways we wouldn't have done otherwise.

I chose these because I had come into the position of associate pastor at Martin with the decision that it was time to grow spiritually. I had always been convinced that the path to God is through love, and by being vulnerable to these folks that I was given to lead, I was choosing to walk that path.

During all of these classes, a couple of phrases kept popping up. One was that we should be intentional about our walk with Christ, and the other was that to truly love others, we had to be present for them. We found how these phrases could move us emotionally and yet be so hard to practice.

DIFFICULTIES FOR LIVING
THE KINGDOM OF GOD ON EARTH

Why is it so hard to live the kingdom of God on earth? It is just easier to practice being intentional about a job or a career than to reinvent oneself as a person. Then there is the part where reinventing ourselves from an "earthly" blueprint isn't what is needed here. If I want to grow as a member of the family of God, then I need a godly blueprint for my new birth. Where do you buy one of these? What about being present? How do we learn to listen with our souls, for that is what being present is all about? It is to hear with our whole selves what someone else is trying to communicate, especially when they don't know what they are trying to say, and we must help them get it out (1 Corinthians 2:10–16). These are things God has revealed to us by his Spirit.

The Spirit searches all things, even the deep things of God. For who knows a person's thoughts except their own spirit within them? In the same way, no one knows the thoughts of God except by the spirit of God. What we have received is not the spirit of the world but the Spirit who is from God which is given so that we may understand what God has freely given to us.

This is what we speak, not in words taught us by human wisdom but in words taught by the Spirit explaining spiritual realities with Spirit-taught words. The person without the Spirit does not accept the things that come from the Spirit of God but considers them foolishness, and we cannot understand them because they are discerned only through the Spirit. The person with the Spirit makes judgments about all things, but such a person is not subject to merely human judgments for "who has known the mind of the Lord so as to instruct Him?" (Isaiah 40:13) However, we must now have the mind of Christ.

Often when someone grasps a concept for the first time, we will say that they "get it." "Getting" the Bible requires that we also "get" love and especially unconditional love. Yes, God's love is more than we can fathom, and yet we can feel it. We can even emulate it if we are willing to throw away all caution and risk loving others without the certainty of getting loved in return. This kind of love is a journey taken a step at a time, and it is the true path to the kingdom of God. (Seek first the kingdom of God [Matthew 6:33].)

How can we know that this is the way? Consider the words of Jesus himself: "A new command I give you. Love one another. As I have loved you, so you must love one another. By this all men will know that you are my disciples, if you love one another." (John 13:34–35) This is his command to us and, like the great commandment, it is God's intent that we should all make this our way of life.

"Love one another. As I have loved you" (John 13:35). With the authority given him by God, the Father, Jesus shows us the central message of the Bible, and what God's intent is for all of his children.

As the leader of those who join with me in study, I am listening to the Spirit as I myself journey in learning to live these phrases from a family-of-God standpoint. In Hebrew, the verb "to hear," especially as it applies to hearing God, includes the understanding that if one hears God's word, then he or she must then do as the word calls us to do. If I hear God calling me to be present for others, then I must make the attempt to do so. A part of God's call on my life is, as I have previously said, to be present for others. I have reflected on this part of God's call on my life, and it has occurred to me that Jesus has shown me the way and given me further guidance on being present for others.

When Jesus was born of Mary and by the Holy Spirit, he brought the kingdom of God into the world. Even as a child speaking in the synagogues, where he went the kingdom went. So the Lord's Prayer, which he gave to the disciples, was already fulfilled in his days as in his person he brought in the kingdom on earth as it was in heaven. He united the kingdom to come with the kingdom now and declared that the two are one. It is, therefore, up to us Christians to let the world know by the way we live that the kingdom is here.

We are the gatekeepers who, by our willingness to walk in the way of Jesus, open the way for these kingdoms to combine in the here and now. They are already combined; we just get to show that they are. And we must also show the way so that others can follow the Holy Spirit and also develop kingdom eyes.

The great commandment (and Jesus's one commandment) to love one another as he loves us is the path to becoming one of his gatekeepers. Love of this sort is noticeable by others and, at the very least, they feel warmed by it. Then, at the most, they feel the presence of God around the one giving such love.

The world is at war with the kingdom of God, which is combined here on earth. Individuals, countries, some Christians and Christian leaders, and some members of other faiths are corrupted by the evil in this world, so that this same evil can further its purpose and hold out against God.

To many people, it seems that evil has already won. Injustices of all kind proliferate in this world, and people and nations refuse to work together for the good of all. Instead, most work on their own in order to gain what they want for themselves. However, God will have his victory even as we fall short of his glory. He will use all that we can give at each juncture of our journeys into him.

"You are from God, little children, and have overcome them because greater is He who is in you than he who is in the world" (1 John 4:4).

> I do not understand what I do. For what I want to do I do not, but what I hate I do… I have the desire to do what is good, but I cannot carry it out… I see another law at work in me, waging war against the law of mind and making me a prisoner to the law of sin at work within me. What a wretched man I am! Who will rescue me from this body that is subject to death? Thanks be to God, who delivers me through Jesus Christ our Lord! (Romans 7:15–20)

REFLECTIONS ON A PAST TIME

I have recently written that listening with our very souls is what we are called to do for others as gatekeepers, and here are some instances where I did and didn't listen well.

- I was playing golf with a church member, and the starter combined us with a really interesting eighty-two-year-old man. He was really pleasant to play with and a much better player than either of us. We had ample opportunity to go further than pleasantries, and yet somehow I just never went there. I feel we could all have gained by simply asking more about this man and then listening to him. I failed to do so, and who knows what was lost as a consequence?

- Before a golf game recently, a friend and I met at a fast-food restaurant, and a man of about my age saw my Vietnam veteran shirt and began to talk to us in a loud voice about his service in Vietnam. My friend wanted to ignore him, and he was in fact being obnoxious, so it would have been easy for me to do so. However, I tried to get past his bluster and visit with him just on a friendly level—to be present. I didn't do so well as he continued to be loud, and I didn't stop and call on the Holy Spirit to help me get past that. It takes practice to listen, especially at the level of being present, and I have far to go.

- On the other hand, I was at my usual place on a Thursday morning for breakfast at a local golf course restaurant. There was a man there who had begun to leave his copy of a national newspaper with me. I guess it was because he sees me reading my local paper and has assumed that I would like
- to read another. Not long ago, he saw me typing on my laptop and asked me what I was writing. A conversation was started, and it soon swung to him and his history. I listened, and because I listened, he is now bringing some ancient coins that he has collected for me to see. All I did was listen, and he felt heard.

Interestingly, my usual waitress stopped by as he left and asked if I knew the man. When I said I didn't, she was shocked and said, "He never talks to anyone." All that I had done before our conversation was to smile and thank him for the papers that he would leave with me.

Concluding Thoughts: Some Things That Have Changed in Me

When I was in my teens and early twenties, I had no real purpose in life, and like many of my generation, I didn't trust folks over thirty years of age. For me, the reason was as much because I couldn't imagine what I would do with myself at that advanced age. I joined the marine corps to buy time and see if they could, indeed, whip me into shape for life.

I was eighteen when I reported to marine corps boot camp in San Diego, California. I was twenty-one when I got out in 1963, and when the Vietnam War broke out, I decided to see if war could make me a man, and I went back into the marines. It was 1965, early in the Vietnam adventure as I thought of it, and I went off to be a soldier of fortune.

I never made it into combat as my MOS (job description) as a radio relay technician was considered too critical to let me go out with the ground troops as a radio operator. There were only a few of us in our battalion and not enough in the whole Third Marine Division. My first sergeant made it clear that I would be court-martialed if I tried to join the recon (reconnaissance) marines in battle.

Therefore, I never got to test myself in battle, but it was there in that zone of battle that I began to question God himself, about his existence and, if he existed, what he was about.

There was that hole in me that I have spoken of, and I began to try and fill it with a God I didn't believe in. Clearly, in retrospect, it was God motivating me to find that he was real, as was his kingdom. My earthly needs were just that—earthly; and he wanted me to look to my heavenly needs for real meaning. I wasn't there yet.

When I got back to the US, my jobs in aerospace were unfulfilling, and after a couple of years and being laid off at LTV in Grand

Prairie, I began my brief career as a singer-musician. It was then that I realized that I thought women were on earth to please men, and at least one was especially here to please me. And, by the way, that didn't work in the reverse. Men weren't here to please women.

I had a very immature, fairy-tale-like idea of love. There was a princess waiting for me and I would find her, sweep her off her feet, and she would make me happy ever after.

Luckily for me and the women I was to meet in this period mostly lasted just for the time I was on the road as an entertainer. God called me in from the darkness and began the arduous task of teaching me to love and value others.

I write this now because I was just in a doctor's office this morning. Jesse and I are wrapping this book up to send off for a hoped-for publication, and while I was in this office, a nice-looking medical assistant came in to interview me.

No, I wasn't immediately attracted to her; rather, I was jolted back to my twenties, remembering my old ways. I could clearly see in that moment how I have changed.

I now see that men and women are meant to please each other only so much as that benefits procreation. For the deeper meaning of life, just pleasing each other will not suffice. It is true that some couples can find a rewarding life with each other, but if they do, it is because they are loving unconditionally at some level.

Most of us have heard some version of the saying: "If you can't love yourself, then you can't love others either." This is a truth that I have tried to dig into on a spiritual level in this book. God wants us to look only to him for our purpose in life. No human on earth can fill us as he can, and now, in my marriage to Suzie, I am constantly called by God to be the giver and not the taker in our relationship.

Most of us know that others can't make us happy. We've heard this ad infinitum, and yet how many of us spend time truly working on bringing heaven to earth by loving others as ourselves.

Here is the change point of my life. I can't fully love this way yet, but I can work at this daily. I don't, of course, work on loving in a kingdom way daily, but I do work at working on it daily. When I fail, I ask God to help me up, dust me off, and help me on my way to that kind of love again. This is the change in me that I hope makes a difference in the world around me. I choose to try and walk on holy ground daily by the power of the Spirit in me, and I pray to God daily and all day for his help. I say to him, "I am nothing and nobody without you, God. Help me to know that my life only has meaning for me and others in those times that I am reaching out to you."

It has come to me, as I have written about my journey into my Lord's kingdom here and beyond, that we humans wield enormous spiritual power. That, of course, is an audacious statement that needs some fleshing out.

Consider this: you go into a crowded room where people are celebrating, and you have no idea about what this is about, but their joyous mood is infectious, and soon you feel elated right along with them.

Or consider this: you go into another crowded room where everyone is in a deeply somber mood. You will be hard-pressed to remain upbeat in such a gathering, although in either room you can go against the prevailing mood if you choose, but it will take a good deal of effort.

I remember going into a church in California when I was a young US marine. It was some form of a Pentecostal service, and I entered at a time when the pastor had the room in the palm of his hands spiritually. Maybe a better term was that he had them hypnotized, but I am quite sure that hypnotism happens at a spiritual level anyway.

I was immediately caught up in the power of that swaying room and felt myself drawn out of all my defenses. I ran from that room as fast as I could and never went back.

It is not for me to judge that way of worshipping. I am just pointing out how we are caught up by the spirit of groups that we are either a part of or in the vicinity of.

Look at the larger scale of our nation's politics. The bitterness and anger of the US government and of the state governments is like an ocean wave rolling over America. We are all caught up in it and in the politics thereof.

Immigration, abortion, monetary policy, war in foreign countries, terrorism, and many more weighty subjects are so reported on that our feelings about them hang in the very air. Our psyches—our very spirits —are bombarded with questions like these and other hot-button subjects, like the environment and warming of the earth. Also, the sexual exploits exposed about many powerful men from the past and the present trouble over our sense of right and wrong.

We are, I believe, spiritual beings, and God's creative power is in us to do good or evil. The conversations that we have within ourselves, and in larger and larger groupings, have spiritual effects on us all. We get to go with the flow of a particular belief system propagated by one group, or we get to go with another in opposition to the first, or we can go in another direction entirely within our minds and spirits.

With all of earth's people crying out with their agendas and beliefs about what is best for us all, is there any wonder that these times are confusing?

I have said that at our soul level, we are lifted up by the Holy Spirit, and at the same time beset upon by the evil spirit of Satan.

There is also such a thing as the soul of a nation and the soul of the world.

At that all-encompassing level, the greater war for the kingdom is raging. We can let ourselves be caught up in national or international arguments and rage with them, or we can call upon God within us to free us from the public fray, its directionality and its spiritual source.

At the simplest level, one person loving God and loving others as themselves brings the kingdom with them everywhere they go. Relatively speaking, when you stand near such a person, you are standing on holy ground.

God is in people who believe in him, be they Christians or of other faiths, to fight against the demonic evils of selfish will at all levels. Evil wants us to destroy us and this world so as to spit in the face of God. Evil will not get his way in the end, but oh the horror he can bring in the meantime!

We wield spiritual power through our thoughts and actions done in love or not. Which will we choose?

When enough of us allow the love of God in us to create enough positive kingdom spiritual energy to push back and defeat evil, we are helping God answer the Lord's Prayer: "Thy will be done, on earth as it is in Heaven" (Matthew 6:9–13).

In this book, I have attempted to make a case for living in the kingdom now—to have kingdom eyes. God created us to work with him for the salvation of ourselves and others—more than just for our own personal salvation. He wants us to move on to sanctification, so as to live and work within his will for the saving of the many.

Paul says this in Romans 12:1–2: "I appeal to you therefore, brothers and sisters by the mercies of God, to present your bodies as a living sacrifice, holy and acceptable to God, which is your spiritual worship. Do not be conformed to this world, but be transformed by the renewing of your minds, so that you may discern what is the will of God—what is good and acceptable and perfect."

Paul also says in 2 Timothy 4:7, "I have fought the good fight, I have finished the race, I have kept the faith."

Athletes in our day speak of leaving it all on the field of play. They call on themselves and their teammates to not hold anything back in their playing of the game—whatever the sport. We watch as some of these football, baseball, basketball, and soccer players, among other sports, train so hard that we wonder if we could ever do as much.

Paul did give that much, and he asks us as players in the grandest drama and game ever whether or not we will do as much as they do. The reward is to know the will of God because we would be just as deeply involved with him and hear him speak to us. "Let anyone with ears to hear listen. Pay attention to what you hear; the measure you give will be the measure you get, and still more will be given to you" (Mark 4:22–25).

THE KINGDOM EFFECT: A GIVER; NOT A TAKER BE
BY JIM VAN RITE

I wrote about how I didn't know how to love. I just didn't get that warm feeling that people describe as one of the attributes of love. I used to lament that the commercial for Schlitz beer, which called for "going for the gusto," as a commentary on my lack. I had no gusto in my life. So I grew angry with God when he didn't fill me with love as soon as I reluctantly accepted his calling me to the ordained ministry. I expected him to do that, and I felt that he had failed me.

Little did know that the kingdom was already working in me. In my second year at Texas Wesleyan College, I married a woman who already had two sons. One of those boys, Jeremy, came to live with us and the other with his father.

As I said, my father never told me that he loved me until he was near his death, and even then, I initiated the conversation. So I decided that any child of mine would never lack hearing those words from me.

I told Jeremy early and often that I loved him. It did feel good to say those words, but the feeling good was not only in the saying. There was freedom in uttering words that my dad couldn't offer me. Freedom didn't equate to love, but I accepted that small gain, and Jeremy wouldn't notice the difference I felt. I was acting like I loved him, so how would he know any difference?

The truth is easy to see now. God didn't point his spiritual finger at me and zap me with loving feelings. Rather, he let me begin developing a bond of love between myself and my stepson that continues strong until this day; and I still never end a time together or a phone call without saying "I love you."

I told my first wife that I loved her also. But even though we both felt that God brought us together, our past histories kept us from fully trusting each other. She was from an alcoholic family, and I was from an equally flawed dysfunctional family. Neither of us had seen modeling of productive communication between spouses. She carried a lot of anger inside her, and then let it explode later, and I muzzled my anger so as not to be like my dad. There came a time when I felt it would be more productive to let my anger out and see if we could be honest with each other. I wanted God in Jesus to help us grow together, and she wanted to explore the Unitarian Church. Financial issues put a stake in the heart of our marriage, and words and deeds of love never got the fertile ground they needed.

I have been shaped down to my soul by saying words that resonated down there deep within me and slowly changed me on the outside also.

The people in the ~~first~~ churches that I served got a sense that I loved them because I always said the words and did my best to act on them. As I look back, I have no doubt that love was finding a foothold in me. However, my emotional growth was achingly slow, and the confusing thing was that I would cry watching sad movies. My eyes would well up with tears when I would read about times when people committed acts of extreme heroism that saved lives or comforted people in dire need of support. How could I have these episodes in which I felt raw emotion and still not have access to everyday feelings of love? I often felt defeated and told God that if he had not failed me, then surely I must have failed him.

As I have said, my first marriage ended because my wife was as wounded as I was when it came to knowing her feelings, and even several years in the "marriage encounter" system as a clergy couple couldn't get us past our distrust of ourselves and each other.

A terrible price was paid by Jeremy and Joshua, my biological son, but my words of love to them kept us close even as both boys struggled to find themselves. The kingdom of God was working on me even as I wondered if God himself even cared.

When Jeremy was invited by his mother to leave home, I had to agree because he said he would not abide by the rules of the household. He was only sixteen years old, and I found it very hard to let go, so I said to him that I would buy his lunch every Tuesday, and we would not talk about negatives. We would just be together.

He eventually had to go to jail and to spend his own time in AA, and then go through many failed relationships before he began to emerge from his fog and begin a productive life.

I was my father's child, and the cycle continued with Jeremy. He didn't know how to love himself or others, but his bond with me remained.

God was at work in both of us in spite of the family burden of being closed off to others.

Joshua had his own dark time. He flirted with gang life and had to spend some time in Alateen, but he emerged and now has a loving family of his own. He and I still don't talk without ending with "I love you."

God has always been there working, and he kept me acting out of love even when I didn't feel it.

There was a time after the divorce from my first wife that I wrote prodigiously, letter after letter to her that never got mailed. Then I took a chance with a woman I met, and I went all in with the "I love yous" and acting in loving ways toward her. She was in an abusive relationship and couldn't get out of it, but I also wrote more letters to her that I never mailed.

I felt the love. All the acts of love with my boys, church members, and even with my first wife were bearing on me as I was again applying the work of doing love to myself and others, and the feeling of love began to emerge in me.

God and the kingdom were at work in me.

When I met Suzie, I had already experienced the risk that comes with being vulnerable with a woman who had always been in abusive relationships. That relationship had no chance, but through it, I learned that I could survive dropping walls between me and others. I even began to have access to the everyday feelings that I had fought with God about for so many years. So, I stepped away from her for both of our sakes.

So, Suzie and I started with a more complete me. I wasn't emotionally and spiritually well yet, but I found it easy to open up to her now that I knew I could. She was able to be open to me also. I learned that we were not so different and that she had the same problem loving self and others that I had. So one night I told her that she couldn't love me as she didn't love herself. She also had trust issues that I felt would be hard to overcome.

Her answer brought me up against what I call "an eternal moment." She said, "Let me love you as best I can." My whole life before that moment and my hopes for a better life going forward came into a sharper focus. This was a decision about my eternal soul as much as anything. Here was my chance to risk all on God healing us both. I could go and lose this chance, or I could stay and, as I would later say, "journey together." (She says, "Walk our path together.")

I had one of those waking-up dreams the next morning of just that—Suzie and I walking into eternity together. Later we would speak of our journey and path. My only question was "Could she really grow past her trust issues and her own poor self-image and learn to give herself over to love?" My answer came quickly. I just quickly felt assured that God had gotten us to that point, and he would always be with us going forward.

God and the kingdom were at work in us.

We had both acted in loving ways to each other, and the die was cast.

Shortly after Suzie and I got together, she joined the ladies auxiliary of the VFW, and I joined the VFW. I joined only because I saw a chance to serve our veterans. I knew by then that my actions in loving others made a difference in me.

I was warmed by spearheading the feeding of homeless veterans using money available from the state office of the VFW and later organizing deployment parties and homecoming parties for our Texas National Guard troops going and coming from Iraq.

I started using this phrase: "A giver, not a taker, be." (I am not sure of its origin, but a Google search failed to find an exact match.) I had learned that the warm reward of giving without expecting something in return was a major stepping-stone on the journey/path that Suzie and I wanted to take together. The great commandment came to mind (Matthew. 22:36–40). I saw the act of giving unconditionally as being a major way to build my spiritual house on a stone foundation. The phrase, "A giver, not a taker, be" has become a favorite of mine— whatever its origin.

Recently, I heard a spouse saying something that I often heard at the departure parties. She said, "My heart swells with pride at what my husband is doing, and still I fear how I would take it if he doesn't come back." She also said, "How would I tell my kids?" A year later, when we welcomed those same soldiers home, I had the experience of spending time with the families under a program offered by the army. That program is called Military OneSource. Suzie and I, along with other members of our VFW post, laughed and cried and were just there for the families of our deployed troops.

With permission from the commanding officer of the headquarters company, I also maintained a website that let me highlight some of what the troops were doing and forward to them what their families were doing to support each other while they (the troops) were in harm's way. My heart was stretched.

I am a singer, and back then I hosted karaoke shows. When I would sing John Michael Montgomery's song "Letters from Home" or Trace Adkins's "I Made It to Arlington" (National Cemetery), I would tear up all over again.

God and the Kingdom were working in me.

We at the VFW also served holiday meals to homeless veterans for several years. I had garnered funds from our VFW's state headquarters to make this possible, and this was another thing that swelled our hearts.

After all of this, I could still be pretty stiff around strangers, and Suzie and our friends made it their loving task to open me up. They have done a fairly good job on me because now, when I meet people coming and going, I make a point to greet them as warmly as I can. It changes me still.

Love is a gift that just keeps on giving.

After Suzie and I got together, I felt moved to get back in church, and we began to attend St. Andrews UMC in Arlington, Texas. Later, when we wanted to be closer to friends and a VFW post we had joined, we moved to Hurst, Texas, and began attending William C. Martin UMC, where I later joined the staff as associate pastor. A woman in one of the after-hours classes that I organized at Martin UMC put her hand on my chest after an evening class I taught and said to me that she felt God's spirit on me. Me, the guy who had been so selfish for so many years…yes, me, who had prayed for God to lead me out of my selfishness. I was able to tell those who took my class that I loved them. They knew that I meant it. All I had to do was to risk doing the love. My prayers were answered. Others felt God's love—even his spirit—in me.

I told the class that when we do loving and kind things over time, we become loving and kind people. I was just acting on what I was teaching. God was with me to do this.

I also told the class that by trying to act out God's love, we begin to see the possibility of getting a grasp on the words of Jesus. His challenging words can seem so far beyond us. How can we love our enemies or forgive them? Can we really love others in the way Jesus loves us? For me, just loving the person next to me was the problem, and yet I was really feeling that love; moreover, they were feeling my love for them also.

Could it really be that simple? Act on love and be loving?

Does Jesus really feel more approachable to us as we invest in loving others? That is a large part of what kingdom eyes is about. Our blindness is healed, and our ears are opened to his call when we risk saying and doing loving things.

Am I healed of my selfishness and self-centeredness? No, but I am out of intensive care and getting more and more well spiritually. I am further into the kingdom than only a few short years ago.

Since I retired again from professional ministry, we have left Martin UMC and are now attending First UMC in Euless, Texas.

Sometimes I teach Sunday school, and in a recent class, I taught that honest communication requires us to be vulnerable. If we can't be honest about who we are, then real communication is stymied.

So I told the class about my history of being closed to others, and I invited my wife, Suzie, to share her first impression of me. She told them that she thought that I was the most arrogant person she had ever met. Now she tells anyone who cares to listen that she and I talk about everything. We share our love in our openness with each other.

Several in the class expressed fear at being honest and open with others. I admitted that it can be dangerous if we feel that we have something to hide, but I told them that I have stopped being the gatekeeper to my feelings and instead have asked God to be my protector.

Some secrets shouldn't be aired out publicly or for all to hear, but it is spiritually unhealthy to keep them locked inside ourselves. God, and hopefully a trained counselor or at least a best friend, should be trusted with our most innermost struggles. So, however we let ourselves be opened, the Holy Spirit should be trusted. He will free us from the wall that self-protection puts between us and others.

For example, publicly forgiving someone who has hurt us puts the burden back on them in a loving way. Will they accept our forgiveness and be healed themselves? Or will they be embarrassed and hang onto their anger? The possibility for healing has been put on the table, and great healing for both of us is now possible. God can lead us to offer the healing, and we can hope that he can reach the other also.

I have modeled being vulnerable with our Sunday school class by sharing as much about me as is healthy for me and them. As I said above, if the need is there to share more deeply, a professional counselor would be appropriate. Prayer and meditation are helpful for all, and some can benefit with just those. However, some people need more. I have sought out counseling before and leave that door open. I would hope that others do also.

Either way, the Spirit is always there to hear us, whether we know it or not.

The class members have my example, and some have thanked me for it. They and others admit they are still fearful of being vulnerable, but at least the subject has been broached.

Honest communication has been held up as the way to healthy relationships, and Suzie and I are willing to be in the spotlight.

Once again, being open and loving to others is the way to walk into the kingdom way. Greeting others with a smile that comes out of our love for God is a way to invite others to that same walk.

For several years now, I have said to God that without him, I am nothing and nobody. By this, I mean that my relationship with him through Jesus is the source of my identity. He is my compass that gives me direction without which I would not know whether to turn right or left in life. He guides my thoughts day and night so that I can know where to search for answers on how to think and how to live.

He encourages me through the Holy Spirit to do love so that my very soul/my self is enriched with a sense of conviction that I am going in the right direction. He opens me to thoughts and ideas that I wouldn't otherwise have.

My conversations with God as a result of acknowledging him as my compass cause me to do for others and for the church things like visiting the ill, teaching what he puts on my heart, and greeting others with his love. I see and feel the kingdom around me as my primary reality. The world's values at best try to rise to the level of the kingdom, but we fight over what is the best way for us to live. In the middle of this fight are the poor and downtrodden that Jesus championed. I am being changed so I can feel the pain of those who have less. How can I be effective in easing their pain? My and Suzie's giving is only a beginning.

I see those who demonstrate the love of God through their actions. I see people who give to the poor with time, money, and love through programs for disadvantaged schoolchildren, and I feel that I am standing on holy ground when near them.

Suzie and I talk of expectations—often of those she puts on herself about pleasing me. I have spent much time in prayer about this, and so I can tell her that my need is for her to be okay with herself and not with pleasing me. If I expect things from her, then I am not able to love unconditionally. I am *conditioning* my love for her on how she does for me. That is unhealthy love, and we have discussed this on many occasions. I want her to feel uplifted by my love, and I want my love for her to feel like an extension of the love of God. In this way, it is my hope that she will look beyond me to a deeper trust in God's love. She spent all her life before we met feeling less than and untrusting of others. Even her love for God couldn't free her to feel herself as someone worthy of his or anyone's love. I want her to have the freedom to feel herself loved, and I attempt to give her that love daily. I just want her to know that God is the source of my love and that I need for it to be that way as much as she does.

CONCLUSION

What each of us believes to be real is based on where we stand culturally and the kind of lens through which we look at the world. Kingdom eyes, as I described them, are gained in the walk from justification to sanctification. The doing of love and forgiveness that Jesus taught and commanded is what causes us to be able to focus on the otherwise unseeable kingdom of God.

Our kingdom vision is sharpened when we start to walk the narrow road of giving up our will and, indeed, our very knowledge of who we are for a new identity in Christ.

Modern conservative Christians have decided to look through the lens of politics and law and believe that this country and its government need to be ruled by God. This is called a theocracy and is what the Jews had among themselves in the Days of Jesus on earth. It is what Iran has today. They misused their authority and abused God's people in the name of God. They didn't or really wouldn't hear Jesus quoting Isaiah on setting the captives free or freeing the oppressed (Luke 4:18–19). Nor did they hear the words of Micah 6:8: "He has shown you man what is good; and what does the Lord require of you, but to do justly, to love mercy, and to walk humbly with your God."

The Jews' mistakes are repeated within that part of the conservative church that wants to go to religious war against all who disagree with them, thus killing the spirit of Jesus within the church.

Love, grace, and compassion are dead or dying within these churches as they declare war on those marginalized by race, sexual orientation, or by who they marry, and yes, this is especially true for those who are poor and not white.

It is time for those of us who see the world through kingdom eyes to stand against these false prophets and show America and the world what it means to free the oppressed through God's enduring love for us all.

ABOUT THE AUTHOR

Mr. Van Rite is an ordained United Methodist elder (retired). His BS degree is from Texas Wesleyan University (then Texas Wesleyan College), and he got his MDiv from Brite Divinity School at TCU.

He spent ten years as a full-time UMC pastor, with some success, but then chose to take "honorable location" while he worked out some family problems. Divorce came anyway, and he was out of the church professionally for twenty-five years. The book was always calling to him because the Holy Spirit, as it does for us all, continued to work in his life.

After meeting his second wife, Suzie, Mr. Van Rite began teaching Sunday school at St. Andrews UMC in Arlington, Texas.

While a tenant of AA, he heard the quote "Feelings follow action" and decided that if it worked for others, it just might work for him. It did. He felt a great need to surrender to God, and he and his family moved to Hurst, Texas, where he was offered the position of associate pastor at Martin UMC in Bedford, Texas.

Six years later, he decided to retire, and for the first time since seminary, writing this book became possible.

"A beautiful exploration and exposition of awareness in action...You express it so clearly and thoroughly."
-Jessica Zeller, Transpersonal psychotherapist, Founder, Natural Pathways Foundation,

"From a place of embodied knowing- your yes can be a yes, without hesitation or doubt. When you know something at the body level, it is deeply rooted, whereas knowing in the mind is prone to fluctuation. And yes, creation has also become my beloved. The pulse of creation is alive in and as us- and it is absolutely an open allowing which allows the most complete unfolding of what is wanting to express. Well said!"
-Sarah J McDonnell, Founder Embodied GLOW

"This is deep, compelling writing. I appreciate you sharing where your journey of introspection with no assumptions has led you. And it shines the light on what the rest of us can do, step by step, building over time, to discover truths. This is especially useful when it thwarts "common wisdom" or penetrates the language of ideas already existing on a "good life". Keep going!"
-Daniel Levitt, Founder, Exember

"Beautifully (and soulfully) written, Holly!"
-Andrea Weinfurter, Founder Momenti Leadership Group

"You are a profound, insightful channel - a seer and builder of creation from Spirit."
-Roger Baril, Founder of Biokinetics

"Radical Wholeness Field Notes brings immediate clarity, coherence, and relief. It offers a precise and compassionate framework for understanding human experience without pathologizing it, revealing healing as a return to the integrity beneath adaptation and protection. Deeply accessible and quietly liberating, these writings remind us that nothing is fundamentally broken and that wholeness has never been lost, only obscured."
-Micheline Green, Founder Rising Together Academy, Author Leadership Parenting

"Radical Wholeness: Field Notes is an intimate companion to Holly Woods' seminal Radical Wholeness Primer. It takes us into the author's interior journey from fragmentation to wholeness. Those willing to take this journey can expect to meet life differently because they are no longer divided inside. From this place of Radical Wholeness, new possibilities emerge as we become available to the creative power of Love that animates our world."
-Ross Hostetter, Author of Keepers of the Field: An Invitation to the Unitive Life.

"This writing is so relevant to what so many people are experiencing today. It is far deeper than just dealing with behavior or what we think we need to heal. Your work is on the leading edge of what humanity needs now to awaken. The world will not change until we do. Thank you, one more time, for your courage in sharing and the wisdom with which you have created the Living Portal."
-Don McCrea PhD, Founder, Your Business Legacy, Author, Wisdom-Centered Leadership

"Holly, this lands very much with me. Your coherence/fragmentation frame articulates something I see daily in senior professionals: the exhaustion isn't from the workload—it's from the internal negotiation that precedes every decision. Effort amplifying fragmentation rather than resolving it. That's the mechanism most burnout interventions completely miss."
-Teresa Hand-Campbell, Founder, Total Human Capital Consultancy